D0327014

A5

EARLY EPIC SCENERY

Homer, Virgil, and the Medieval Legacy

By the same author

The Icelandic Family Saga: An Analytic Reading

The Problem of Icelandic Saga Origins: A Historical Survey

Co-editor with Larry D. Benson, *The Literary Context of Chaucer's Fabliaux: Texts and Translations*

Early Epic Scenery

Homer, Virgil, and the Medieval Legacy

THEODORE M. ANDERSSON

CORNELL UNIVERSITY PRESS

ITHACA AND LONDON

First published 1976 by Cornell University Press.
Published in the United Kingdom by Cornell University Press Ltd., 2–4 Brook Street, London W1Y 1AA.

Passages from *P. Vergili Maronis Opera*, edited by R. A. B. Mynors, are reprinted by permission of Oxford University Press, Oxford.
Passages from *Beowulf* are reprinted by permission of the publisher from *Beowulf and the Fight at Finnsburg*, 3d ed., edited by Fr. Klaeber (Lexington, Mass.: D. C. Heath and Company, 1950).

International Standard Book Number 0–8014–1013–4
Library of Congress Catalog Card Number 76–12593
Printed in the United States of America by Vail-Ballou Press, Inc.
Librarians: Library of Congress cataloging information appears on the last page of the book.

ৡ❧

Preface

The following essay has gone through a considerable metamorphosis, beginning as a restricted study of one Germanic text and expanding into a somewhat broader consideration of several European epics. It originated as a speculation on the old question of Virgilian influences in *Beowulf.* Some years ago it struck me that, quite aside from possible reminiscences in phraseology, *Beowulf* showed a special scenic affinity to the *Aeneid,* a manner of visualizing epic action that is foreign to Germanic poetry and comprehensible only with reference to Virgil. This observation led to a series of tests. First it was necessary to define the scenic similarities, then to determine whether they are significant, that is, whether the *Beowulf* poet in fact modeled his practice on the *Aeneid* or simply shared habits that are universal in epic poetry. The inquiry thus widened into a definition of Virgil's scenic technique in terms of his own tradition, primarily the Homeric epic. Once Virgil's contribution to the development of epic scenery was isolated, the next question to be answered was whether his scenic principles were imitated in the early Middle Ages. Certain Carolingian pieces clearly revealed this type of imitation and made it plausible that the *Beowulf* poet, writing at roughly the same period, could have received similar impulses. Finally, the Virgilian analogies in *Beowulf* were underscored by contrasting them to the scenic poverty in the Old French *Roman d'Eneas* and vernacular romance generally. The scarcity of scenic image in these works confirmed that Virgil's manipulation of space was a unique poetic technique bequeathed to a specifically Virgilian school and not a ubiquitous phenomenon to be found at random in narrative poetry.

In the course of these experiments, *Beowulf* began to recede into the background and remains in the final version only as a sort of pendant to the Carolingian chapter. The earlier sections grew, and the essay turns out to be more about Virgil than I had originally envisioned. I now hope that the somewhat extended treatment of epic scenery may offer something of interest to the general student of narrative who is not necessarily concerned with the particulars of the *Beowulf* controversy.

In an effort to make the material as accessible as possible, I have provided translations of all texts quoted in the original. The translations are my own, not for the sake of accuracy or elegance, but of uniformity. I have, on reflection, omitted quotations in Greek, partly to save the cost of printing them and partly because anyone with an interest in the original will have his Homer within easy reach.

The manuscript was largely completed under the generous auspices of the John Simon Guggenheim Memorial Foundation during the year 1972–1973. Most of the writing was done in the library of the American Academy in Rome, and I am deeply grateful to the director, Bartlett H. Hayes, Jr., and to the chief librarian, Nina Longobardi, for their warm hospitality during my stay. Among the colleagues who generously placed their learning at my disposal at various times, I am particularly indebted to Mark Morford, who spent an inordinate part of his sabbatical in Rome answering my questions, without, of course, contracting any responsibility for the ones I failed to ask. For counsel and encouragement I am also indebted to my Virgil of long standing, Larry D. Benson.

T. M. A.

Cambridge, Massachusetts

Contents

Editions Cited

Iliad	*Homeri Opera.* I–II. Ed. David B. Monro and Thomas W. Allen. 3d ed. Oxford: Clarendon, 1920; rpt. 1966 and 1962.
Odyssey	*Homeri Opera.* III–IV. Ed. Thomas W. Allen. 2d ed. Oxford: Clarendon, 1917; rpt. 1965 and 1966.
Aeneid	*P. Vergili Maronis Opera.* Ed. R. A. B. Mynors. Oxford: Clarendon, 1969.
Karolus Magnus et Leo Papa	*Karolus Magnus et Leo Papa: Ein Paderborner Epos vom Jahre 799.* Mit Beiträgen von Helmut Beumann, Franz Brunhölzl, Wilhelm Winkelmann. Paderborn: Bonifacius-Druckerei, 1966.
In Honorem Hludowici	*Ermold le noir: Poème sur Louis le pieux et épîtres au roi Pépin.* Ed. Edmond Faral. Paris: Société d'édition "Les Belles Lettres," 1932.
Waltharius	*Monumenta Germaniae Historica: Poetae Latini Medii Aevi.* VI, 1. Ed. Karl Strecker. Weimar: Hermann Böhlaus Nachfolger, 1951.
Beowulf	*Beowulf and the Fight at Finnsburg.* Ed. Fr. Klaeber. 3d ed. Boston: D. C. Heath, 1950.
Roman d'Eneas	*Eneas: Roman du XIIe siècle.* Ed. J.-J. Salverda de Grave. Paris: Librairie Honoré Champion, 1964–1968.
Tristan	Gottfried von Strassburg. *Tristan und Isold.* Ed. Friedrich Ranke. 9th printing. Zurich and Berlin: Weidmannsche Verlagsbuchhandlung, 1965.

EARLY EPIC SCENERY

Homer, Virgil, and the Medieval Legacy

Latent Space in the Homeric Epics

The *Iliad*

The European epic characteristically involves its heroes in a journey or a series of wanderings. Sea voyages occupy a central position in the *Odyssey*, Apollonius' *Argonautica*, Virgil's *Aeneid, Beowulf,* Camoens' *Lusiads,* and Ronsard's *Franciade,* while overland marches shape the course of Lucan's *Pharsalia,* the *Waltharius,* the *Cid, The Song of Roland,* the *Nibelungenlied,* and Tasso's *Jerusalem Delivered.* With the advent of chivalric romance, narrative form and spiritual search merge in an ever-expanding succession of quests, from Chrétien to Ariosto to Tennyson. It is not surprising that the epic form, which must contend with the danger of monotonous action as well as monotonous diction, should resort to displacements, exotic scenery, or a general sense of restlessness to bind the reader's attention. What is surprising, in retrospect, is that the first and unsurpassed example of the epic genre should refrain from such scenic diversification. The *Iliad* confines its 15,683 verses doggedly to the plain of Troy, going no further afield than Priam's palace on one side and the Greek camp on the other. A few flitting visits to Olympus scarcely detract from this unity since the eyes of the gods are almost always trained on the Trojan action. We might therefore expect to be richly informed about the single scene of this momentous clash, but on inspection the detail turns out to be meager indeed. S. E. Bassett once noted that Homer tells us more about the setting of Polyphemus' cave in the *Odyssey* than he does about the Greek camp or the Trojan plain in the whole of the *Iliad,* and to this we might add that he tells us more of Eumaeus' steading (*Od.* 14. 5–22) than of Priam's palace.[1]

The modern reader is accustomed to having the scene of historical or fictional action elaborated in advance. He is thus enabled to focus the action against a background that he can readily visualize. This is not so in the *Iliad.* Homer plunges the reader (or listener) not only into mid-action, but also into mid-scene, providing only gradually, and quite incidentally, a few details from which the Trojan setting can be pieced together in part. These indications, never full or descriptive, amount to no more than points of reference to which fragments of the action are loosely attached.

We are not given a plan of Priam's palace or an understanding of its position in the city. We have no real perception of the distances on the plain between city and camp. We know that the camp is fortified with a trench and a wall, in which there is a gate, but the exact arrangement is unclear and there are notorious difficulties about the wall, this "curiously impermanent piece of Trojan scenery."[2] Within the camp the action takes place "at the ships," or "at the tents," or "at the ships and the tents," but again the exact arrangement is elusive. We know that Odysseus occupies the center while Achilles and Ajax

[1] Samuel E. Bassett, *The Poetry of Homer,* Sather Classical Lectures 15 (Berkeley: University of California Press, 1938), p. 91.

[2] T. B. L. Webster, *From Mycenae to Homer,* 2d ed. (London: Methuen, 1964), p. 252.

occupy the extremities of the line of ships drawn up on the beach, but whether the line is in one or more ranks, or whether it is straight or curved, is a problem that sometimes excited a heated debate in the last century.[3] The location of the tents relative to the ships is uncertain. Casual hints indicate that the tents are on the same parallel line with the ships and interspersed among them, but this deduction cannot be made before Book xvii and must be reasoned out. The situation is not visualized, and no reader of the *Iliad* will be able to diagram the camp without undertaking a special analysis.

The greater part of the action takes place on the plain, and here too the reader is given only sparse and poorly visualized spatial indications. There are the rivers Simois and Scamander, an oak tree, a wild fig tree, a rise, springs, the tomb of Ilos surmounted by a pillar, a lookout post, and a wagon road. But these items are introduced more or less one at a time between vii. 19–22 and xxii. 145–66 and are not spatially interrelated. I doubt whether the reader is given enough information to plot them on a map even by deduction. When Ovid's fictive Ulysses marks out the Trojan plain on the sand of the seashore for Calypso's entertainment (*Ars Amandi* 2. 131–38), he is providing information that cannot be gleaned from the *Iliad*.

Within a decidedly impressionistic framework two types of scenes are acted out, mass battle or assembly scenes and small group scenes with dialogue. These two categories confront the poet with distinct sets of problems, and it will repay us to study them separately.

The mass scenes pose the dual problem of extended space and simultaneous action. The poet's parsimonious

---

[3] See, for example, W. Ribbeck, "Homerische Miscellen," *Rheinisches Museum für Philologie,* 35 (1880), 610–26 (esp. 614–23).

treatment of space should be apparent from what has been said already, and Zielinski stated seventy-five years ago the difficulties Homer encountered in dealing with simultaneous action.[4] The text does not always bear close scrutiny in these matters, but on the whole we will see that Homer solves both basic problems in a peculiarly satisfactory way. The solution for the wide battle front is simply to ignore it and not to encumber the narrative with spatial discriminations. Information not given need not be accounted for, and the reader is free to imagine whatever location he chooses for any particular phase of the battle action, or he may imagine none at all. The solution for depicting simultaneous action is to portray it only in broadest outline and to a large extent metaphorically. This Homer can do, without loss of vigor or color, through the use of extended similes.

However satisfying in general, these solutions are purchased only at the expense of some disconcerting details. We may consider the following characteristic passages. In Book v, Diomedes' ferocious onslaught carries all before it and we are borne along by his prowess, but a close look reveals that he is operating in a kind of charmed insulation, dispatching Trojans singly or in pairs with no perceptible interference from the crush of battle about him. A case in point is the segment following his slaying of Priam's sons Echemmon and Chromios. At this moment he comes to the attention of Aineias, who does not close on him at once, but goes off among the battlelines in search of Pandarus, "if perchance he might find him" (v. 168). When he does find and address Pandarus, it becomes clear that he has not recognized Diomedes because he bids his

[4] Thaddaeus Zielinski, "Die Behandlung gleichzeitiger Ereignisse im antiken Epos," *Philologus: Zeitschrift für das classische Alterthum*, Supplementband 8 (Leipzig, 1899–1901), pp. 407–49.

companion take aim at "whomever it is who prevails and
inflicts much evil on the Trojans" (v. 175–76). Although
Aineias has been unable to recognize his prominent foe
and appears to have moved even farther away from him,
Pandarus promptly identifies Diomedes by his shield, helmet, and horse. After some dialogue devoted to strategy,
Aineias and Pandarus mount a chariot and charge. As they
approach their foe, they are in turn identified by Sthene-
los, who warns Diomedes of the impending attack, of
which he apparently has been unaware. Throughout this
sequence it is unclear what distances and vantage points
are involved, to what extent, if at all, vision and motion
are impeded by the surrounding mass of troops, and why
identification is sometimes possible and sometimes not.

A similar example of insulated battle action occurs at
the beginning of Book VIII when the Greeks, routed by
Zeus's thunder, turn and flee. Only Nestor is unwillingly
left behind because Paris has struck down one of his horses
with an arrow. While the old man struggles to cut away
the bridle and reins of the dead horse, Hector suddenly
materializes and charges him. Diomedes sees Nestor's
plight and appeals to Odysseus—with Hector presumably
closing the gap rapidly. But Odysseus has joined the flight
to the ships and is deaf to the appeal. Diomedes must
therefore rush to the rescue himself; he does so, apostro-
phizing Nestor in a long and not altogether apposite speech
(VIII. 102–11), while Hector continues to approach in full
career. Then the action is suddenly reversed. Nestor
mounts Diomedes' chariot and they wheel to charge Hector,
who, miraculously, still has not arrived on the scene. The
situation is impossible to visualize. There is something of
the merry-go-round vehicle about Hector's chariot since
it makes no headway. Even allowing for this suspended

time, it is difficult to understand why Nestor is not swamped by the rest of the Trojan soldiery. Finally, it is unclear how Diomedes can run against the tide with perfect impunity if the Greeks really are in total retreat and the Trojans therefore in total advance all along the line.

When, on occasion, distances or directions are specified, they have no binding force. Thus in Book XI Ajax storms about the battlefield out of sight of Hector, who is fighting on the left wing by the banks of the Scamander (XI. 498–99). But just a few lines later Cebriones stands next to Hector and advises an attack on Ajax, whom he readily recognizes (XI. 526) by his body shield. Visibility apparently is determined not by scenic factors but by the poet's arbitrary discretion.

Even after the action has closed in on the Greek ships and therefore become simplified and confined, the scene remains blurred. For example, it is not clear why, when the fighting is swirling all about the ships, Achilles' contingent should remain unaffected. The Trojans might wish to avoid such a confrontation so as not to jeopardize Achilles' aloofness, but the point is never made. Achilles' own position is uncertain; sometimes his view of the proceedings is excellent and sometimes it is completely obscured. He sees the first flames of the ignited ships (XVI. 124–25), and we are told later that he stands in front of his tent to observe the battle (XVI. 255–56), but since the story requires that he not learn of Patroclus' death directly, he fails to see this, the most central fact of the battle (XVII. 377–80, 402). The paradox is so striking that Homer offers a special explanation and injects a supernatural agency: Zeus blots out the scene by shrouding Patroclus in darkness (XVII. 268–70, 366–69).

Normally, the point of maximum pressure and minimum mobility in a battle is the center where the opposing ranks collide. Homer's account shows no such constraint; special actions are assigned precisely to this part of the field, where they are allowed to proceed without hindrance. The memorable encounter between Diomedes and Glaucus takes place when they "came together between the two battle lines eager to fight" (vi. 120). Fighting would be well enough, but what actually occurs is a voluble exchange of courtesies in which the speakers are quite oblivious to the surrounding maelstrom of hostilities. Similarly, during the intense action of Book xi Hector is at liberty to drive his chariot "between the Trojans and the Achaeans" (xi. 533), as if the sea of battle on either side were content to recede and let him pass.

Difficult as it is for the reader to form an exact picture of these engagements, he will find no indication that those on the scene enjoyed any great advantage in this respect. Achilles' imperfect view of the battlefield during the struggle over Patroclus' body is symptomatic. There is small evidence that anyone in either contingent avails himself of the walls of Troy or the fortifications of the Greek camp to survey the action and form an overall impression of the fighting. Unsurveyability is such an inherent feature of the epic that when Hector sets watch fires at the conclusion of Book viii (509–11) to prevent the Greeks from escaping unseen onto their ships during the night, this suddenly extended perspective catches us by surprise—we had no previous reason to suppose that the two camps were visible to one another. Indeed, they seem hardly to be surveyable within their own confines if we are to judge from the words of Agamemnon, who fears that he and Menelaus may miss one another "for there are many paths through the camp" (x. 65–66).

When a wider perspective opens up, it serves no scenic purpose. In XXI. 526–29 Priam has a clear view of Achilles and the action around him from the wall of Troy:

> The old man Priam stood on the divine tower
> And watched hulking Achilles; and before him
> The Trojans were driven, clustered in flight,
> And manifested no courage.

This is the extent of the description because, as we will observe elsewhere, the point is not what Priam sees, but what he feels (XXI. 529–30):

> Groaning he descended from the tower,
> Urgently addressing the excellent gatekeepers by the wall.

The indifference to perspective is signaled again at the beginning of the following book when Priam once more looks out over the battle, with no indication that he has regained the favorable vantage point of the tower. Here his impression of the scene is limited to a simile in which Achilles' appearance is compared to Orion in the night sky (XXII. 26–31). Again, the point is not the scene itself, but the emotion provoked by it (XXII. 33–34):

> The old man groaned, he struck his head with his hands,
> Lifting them high, and, groaning aloud, he cried out. . . .

When Hector is finally slain, his mother and father are apparently witnesses, but their view is not described, only their grief (XXII. 405–09). Andromache is mercifully spared the scene of the killing and arrives on the wall just in time to see her husband dragged off to the Greek ships (XXII. 462–65).[5]

---

[5] John A. Scott, *The Unity of Homer*, Sather Classical Lectures 1 (Berkeley: University of California Press, 1921), pp. 214–15.

The most obvious compensation for this lack of an overview is the frequent resort to Olympus, where the gods
look down on the field of battle from their lofty perspective. In VII. 443–44 they observe the building of the
Achaean wall. In VIII. 198–200 Hera casts a wrathful eye
on Hector as he is about to attack Nestor and Diomedes.
In XI. 80–83 Zeus sits apart from the gods "watching the
city of the Trojans and the ships of the Achaeans, the
flashing of bronze, and men killing and dying." Again in
XI. 336–37 he regulates the battle "looking down from
Ida." But in XIII. 1–16 Zeus averts his eyes and Poseidon
looks down on the battle "from the highest summit of
woody Samothrace." In XIV. 153–60 Hera observes Poseidon's intervention "from the peak of Olympus" and determines to aid his cause by beguiling Zeus. But at the outset
of Book XV Zeus awakens to control the action once again.
In XV. 377–78 he thunders his approval of Nestor's prayer,
in XVI. 567–68 he envelops Sarpedon in darkness, and in
XVII. 198–208 he sees and censures Hector's conquest of
Achilles' armor. In XX. 22–25 he releases the gods to engage in the fray as they see fit, "but I will remain sitting
on the cleft of Olympus, from where I will look on and
rejoice in my heart." Then in XX. 136–37 Poseidon advises
that they sit down apart "in a lookout place." In XXII. 166
the gods witness Hector being dragged three times around
the city. We might assume that this constant view from
above would provide some focus on the battlefield. It
never does. There is no effort to chart positions or events;
the fact of the observation is merely stated and the reac-
tions of the gods are then detailed in direct discourse.

Homer's method is to provide the reader with a large,
blank canvas, on which, as time goes on, he enters a few
items here and there, more or less at random. There is no
general design on which we may rely in following the

progress of the narrative. As a result, we are occasionally
confronted with the presupposition of knowledge we do
not have. When we learn from Dolon's revelations in x.
415 that Hector has convened his councilors "by the tomb
of Ilos," this means very little to us since Ilos' tomb has
not previously been located on the landscape. Then in xi.
371 we find Paris steadying himself against a pillar on
Ilos' tomb to discharge an arrow; the mention of this pillar
is likely to throw us off stride for a moment because we
have accustomed ourselves to the unadorned tomb of the
previous book. The pillar clearly has no scenic or visual
function at all and is therefore not mentioned until it becomes tactically useful. Finally, in xxiv. 349 Priam drives
by the tomb to the river, although we had no inkling
before this, the last book, that the tomb is near the river,
or, if in fact it is not, how exactly the two relate to each
other. The neglect of the setting goes even further. The
authority on Trojan topography, Walter Leaf, felt obliged
to footnote the passage: "Presumably they cross the river
at the ford." [6] But the less experienced reader knows nothing of such a ford since there is no mention of it until
the return trip in xxiv. 692. As a matter of fact, not until
the return trip does Homer identify the river; it turns out
to be the Xanthus (Scamander), though for all we know of
the Trojan plain, it might just as well have been the
Simois.

A further curiosity is the absence of natural features.
The picture we are led to form of the Trojan plain is that
of an arid stretch of flat land. Aside from the mention of a
hillock there is no suggestion of elevation, and the fre-
quency with which dust is kicked up and dust clouds are
mentioned obliges us to imagine that there is a great and
exclusive quantity of this material underfoot. When, there-

[6] Walter Leaf, ed., *The Iliad*, 2d ed. (London: Macmillan, 1902), II, 561.

fore, we read in XXI. 18 that Achilles leans his spear against
a tamarisk or in XXI. 350–52 that Hephaestus consumes a
large number of trees and bushes on the banks of the
Scamander, we may be mildly startled to learn that there
is vegetation along the river.

Homer's indifference to visual aspects of the scene sometimes takes the form of subordinating them to auditory
effects. Characteristic are Agamemnon's impressions as he
gazes at the Trojan watch fires in X. 11–13:

> And when he gazed at the Trojan plain,
> He marveled at the many fires that burned before Troy
> And the shrilling of flutes and pipes and the din of men.

We may note the preponderance of sound (flutes, pipes,
shouts) over sight (fires). The same priority emerges from
an episode in Book XI, in which Odysseus, wounded and
hard pressed by the enemy, brings his plight to the attention of his comrades with an audible rather than a visual
signal (XI. 462–63):

> Three times then he shouted as much as a man's head
>   holds,
> And three times battle-loving Menelaus heard him shout.

Menelaus then turns to Ajax (XI. 466–68):

> The shout of stout-hearted Odysseus has reached me,
> Making it sound as if the Trojans have cut him off
> And are overpowering him in mighty conflict.

To take a familiar analogy, Roland's three blasts on the
horn are readily understandable in view of the distance
separating him from Charlemagne's main force, but Odysseus' three shouts are another matter. If he is too far away
for Menelaus to see, how can he hope to be heard over
what must be the deafening din of general battle? And if

he is not clearly visible, there must be other Greek warriors nearer at hand and in a better position to bring relief. These are, of course, quibbles, but they are indicative of Homer's indifference to scenic detail. Once again in XVIII. 202–29 sight is secondary to sound. Iris bids Achilles appear on the trench to hem the advance of the Trojans, and Athena causes a wondrous flame to issue from his head; its beaconlike visibility is emphasized by an elaborate simile. But when Achilles takes up the required position in plain view of the enemy, the sound of his voice, not the strange sight, throws them into consternation. Only after they have quailed before his shout do they notice the divine flame (XVIII. 225).

Homer once hints that he was aware of the spatial difficulties that confronted him. In the particularly unsurveyable action in Book XII, where the arrangement of wall, gate, and trench is not clear and where the order of the Trojan attack is confused, the poet lets fall the following despondent remark (XII. 176): [7]

> It is difficult for me to account for everything like a god.

The phrasing is varied by Menelaus when he summons the Greek chieftains to recover Patroclus' body in XVII. 252–53:

> It is difficult for me to spy out each of the chieftains,
> So greatly does the contention of arms blaze up.

Neither poet nor participant had an altogether satisfactory view of the battle.

Despite the spotty description of the Trojan plain and an equally spotty description of the action on it, readers

---

[7] On the confused action of Book XII see Richard Heinze, *Virgils epische Technik*, 3d ed. (Leipzig and Berlin: Teubner, 1915; rpt. Darmstadt: Wissenschaftliche Buchgesellschaft, 1957), pp. 223–24. On the force of the line see Zielinski, "Die Behandlung gleichzeitiger Ereignisse," pp. 430–31. Similar lines occur in the *Odyssey* 7. 241–42 and 19. 221–22, the *Aeneid* 2. 361–62, and Milton's *Paradise Lost* 7. 112–14 and 8. 250–51.

are not likely to feel that Homer failed to produce a vivid account. The battle sequences are effective both as a total impression and as a sum of memorable particulars; the poet was successful in compensating for his neglect of visual factors by the use of other effects. Let us first analyze the general impression.

I noted at the outset that the *Iliad* is remarkable among epics because it foregoes the variety afforded by changes of scenery. Yet the action is not uniform or dull. Homer makes abundant use of movement and tension, which on the whole provide greater narrative energy than the scenic variations of the *Odyssey*. The movement is confined to a limited space, but within that space it is more or less constant. There is a perpetual coming and going, an ebb and flow of action across the plain; if one side is not retreating, it is pursuing.[8] This flux is by no means aimless, but takes place within fixed emotional and spatial parameters marked at either extremity by the always imminent threat of total rout on one side or the other. The alternation of panic and desperate rally keeps the reader on edge not because the movement itself is exciting but because it maintains the emotions of the contending warriors at fever pitch.

Although the underlying strain is more important than the surface flow, the latter is not neglected. It is described in a variety of ways through the use of the extended simile. Critics have pointed out that mass movements in the *Iliad* are almost always illuminated by similes; the reason sometimes given is that the simile provides flexibility which relieves the monotony of battle.[9] Another part of the same explanation is that the simile is Homer's solution for deal-

8 Brigitte Hellwig, *Raum und Zeit im homerischen Epos*, Spudasmata 2 (Hildesheim: Georg Olms, 1964), p. 10.

9 C. M. Bowra, *Tradition and Design in the Iliad* (Oxford: Clarendon, 1930), p. 123; G. S. Kirk, *The Songs of Homer* (Cambridge: Cambridge University Press, 1962), pp. 161, 345.

ing with mass scenes, which he cannot otherwise visualize adequately. Hence the *Iliad*'s preponderance of similes in comparison to the *Odyssey* and the fact that four out of five similes in the *Iliad* occur in battle secenes.[10] They serve to highlight the action in a slightly different way each time, depending on whether the movement is likened to flaming woods on mountaintops (II. 455–58), the flocking of birds (II. 459–68), the swarming of flies (II. 469–73), the blowing of leaves or sand across an open space (II. 800–801), the formed flight of screaming cranes (III. 1–7), the rush of black storm clouds (IV. 275–82), the sea breaking on the shore (IV. 422–28), the rushing together of two mountain torrents (IV. 452–56), a flooded stream breaking down dikes and vineyard fences (V. 84–94), the falling of grain before reapers (XI. 67–71), the onslaught of thick snow (XII. 277–89), the contesting of a boundary by aroused neighbors (XII. 421–26), the even balance of scales as a woman weighs wool (XII. 432–35), the pounding of swollen seas on a towering cliff (XV. 618–22), an attack by wasps (XVI. 259–65), or a hunted boar turning to fight off the pursuing dogs (XVII. 722–34). These similes provide such a profusion of motion, design, and acute observation that the reader will hardly feel he is being cheated of visual detail. In all likelihood it is the quality of the similes which prompted such readers as Voltaire and Goethe to admire Homer as a painter of nature even though he has remarkably little to say about the natural setting of his epic.[11]

There is, to be sure, a risk of monotony in the very rush and glare of the action, but Homer guards against the danger in a number of ways, for example through a sparing

---

[10] Bowra, *Tradition and Design*, p. 123.

[11] *Oeuvres complètes de Voltaire*, X (n.p.: L'Imprimerie de la Société Littéraire-Typographique, 1785), 351–52, and *Goethes Werke*, I. 31 (Weimar: Hermann Böhlau, 1904), 238–39; I. 32 (1906), 77; IV. 13 [*Goethes Briefe*] (1893), 66.

but judicious use of contrast. After the catalogue of ships and the great massing of divisions have been tallied in awesome detail, threatening a truly cataclysmic onslaught, the poet turns quite suddenly to the disbanded idleness of Achilles' camp, where his men engage in carefree games by the seashore, the unharnessed horses graze peacefully, and the battle chariots stand unhitched in their tents (II. 771–77). This picture of relaxation after the purposeful marshaling of the Achaeans inverts the narrative mood. A few brief images convey the loss of purpose among Achilles' demobilized Myrmidons as they wander aimlessly about the camp (II. 778–79):

> Missing their war-loving leader,
> They wandered hither and thither through the camp and fought not.

Instead of a richly discriminated panorama the reader is given two brief but vivid glimpses of military life, first the massive discipline of the marshaling and then the oppressive emptiness of military tedium. The emphasis in the contrast is psychological, not scenic.

Surely the most memorable contrast in the poem is the domestic interlude of VI. 369–502 in which Hector and Andromache meet for the last time in Troy.[12] The quiet detail and conjugal harmony are as close as Homer comes to sentimentality, but at the conclusion of the scene he resolutely cuts short the elegiac mood by describing Paris' uncharacteristic and faintly comical eagerness as he "prances from the boudoir to the battle" (VI. 503–17).[13] The opposition in pace and atmosphere in this transition,

[12] That it is the last time is argued by Wolfgang Schadewaldt, "Hektor in der Ilias," in *Hellas und Hesperien: Gesammelte Schriften zur Antike und zur neueren Literatur* (Zurich and Stuttgart: Artemis, 1960), pp. 21–38.

[13] J. B. Hainsworth, *Homer*, Greece & Rome: New Surveys in the Classics 3 (Oxford: Clarendon, 1969), p. 30.

above all the opposition between martial melancholy and
martial high spirits, is symptomatic of Homer's interest in
the currents that run below the surface of the action. The
clash on the battlefield becomes significant against the
background of personalities and personal circumstances.
The characters of Hector and Paris are different, as are
their domestic relations; they therefore enter battle differently and they fight differently. Homer is as attentive to
these individual variations as he is to the great sway of
action.

A quite incidental but characteristic instance of this
balanced outlook occurs in xv. 390–404. As the Trojans
make their final assault on the Greek ships and peril is
stretched to the utmost, Patroclus stops on his way back to
Achilles in order to tend the wound of Eurypylos in his
tent. The gesture may strike us as an imprudent delay at a
crucial moment, but it makes us keenly aware of the variety
of situations and the variety of sometimes conflicting military and personal concerns on the battlefield.

As this last passage illustrates, Homer's tendency to sus-
pend action in an unrealistic way is both a special license
and a special resource of his epic. To take one example, a
prominent feature of Book xvii is that action, even such
relatively brief action as the struggle over Patroclus' body,
may be arrested to allow time for speeches. It is as if everyone involved agrees to certain pauses for dialogue, thus
creating a curious alternation of headlong bursts of activity
and frozen intervals.[14] The freezing can take place at almost absurd moments. In xx. 285–317 Aineias seizes a
stone "which two men, such as are mortal now, could not
lift" and cocks his arm while Achilles is about to strike
with his sword; but at this critical juncture Poseidon and
Hera discuss the impending danger for twenty-seven lines

14 Scott, *The Unity of Homer*, p. 158.

and Poseidon then makes his way to the battlefield to re-
move Aineias. In the meantime the posture of the two
combatants has become statuelike and unreal.

Similarly, in XXI. 324–41 Achilles is seized by a wave as
angry Scamander rushes at him. But at the next moment
we must imagine the wave transfixed and Achilles poised
precariously on the crest while, for the space of eleven
lines, Hera appeals to Hephaestus to intervene. This is
Tennyson's "crest of some slow-arching wave" brought to a
complete standstill. The interruption runs counter to our
experience of continuous action, but for that very reason it
obliges us to stop and absorb a picture we might otherwise
pass over lightly. The contravention of realism is therefore
a device to achieve vividness. Here and elsewhere Homer
constrains our attention by isolating a detail of the action
and obliging us to concentrate on it. The general battle is
not only a picture of colliding masses, as in the similes, but
also a composite of arrested details.

Sometimes the dwelling on detail appears to transport us
into a recalibrated time scheme. Kirk speaks of "the elaborate slow-motion account of the fatal wound." [15] Most
striking is the case of a wound that is not fatal (IV. 112–49).
The description begins with Pandarus' preparations as he
takes aim at Menelaus; it centers not on the larger scene,
or the appearance of the target, or the intervening space,
but entirely on Pandarus' bow and arrow. In other words,
we are asked to focus on only the most immediate of
Pandarus' concerns, to the total exclusion of the peripheral
scene. There follows a description of the hit (IV. 132–40),
a microscopic accounting of the point at which the tip
strikes and a millimetrical measuring of the distance between the first contact with the outer clothing and the ultimate penetration of the flesh. The eye is invited to shift not

15 Kirk, *The Songs of Homer*, p. 342.

so much from Pandarus to Menelaus as from the taut center of Pandarus' concentration to a tiny spot on Menelaus' anatomy. The focus could hardly be narrower. The surrounding action, indeed the very presence of other persons, is lost from view until IV.148–49, when Agamemnon shudders at the sight of his brother's wound. The emphasis is, once again, not on the scene, but only on those participants most directly affected and on their immediate responses.

Far from undertaking an evenly conceived or uniform narrative canvas, Homer limits himself to a blurred sweep of battlescape in which a few figures here and there are dilated and brought into focus. The enlarged areas need not be dramatic, but they are always seen in human rather than scenic terms. Thus, at the outset of the great battle in the central books, Homer does not deploy battle formations, but a single figure: thirty-two lines are given over to a description of Agamemnon's armor (XI. 15–46). It is almost an epic law that the focus shall be directed away from the crowded field, on which we are able to visualize so little, and toward the individual. Even where the frequent verbal adjective παπταίνων ("peering about") occurs, it tends to convey an image of the man who is doing the craning rather than an image of what he sees (XIII. 551, 649; XV. 574; XVII. 84, 115, 603). The most obvious case is XVII. 674–84, a passage in which Menelaus is likened to an eagle darting glances around in search of prey. This description is in line with the general rule that perspectives serve only to illuminate the observer, as in the case of Patroclus' view of the Greek rout (XV. 395–404), a perspective that concedes one line to the actual view, one line to the confusion of battle, and all the rest to Patroclus' groan, the smiting of his thighs, and his anguished soliloquy.

Patroclus himself is revealed to us, not the tide of battle, which acquires a degree of reality only through the medium of Patroclus' perceptions.[16]

Bassett made the point that in mass scenes or familiar surroundings Homer pays no heed to the setting, whereas in scenes limited to a single individual or a small group, he makes some allowance for the environment.[17] This practice is in keeping with the narrow Homeric focus. But even within a narrowed range, the descriptive resources remain meager. The most frequent pattern involves a conversation between two persons whose arrival on the scene is never detailed and whose meeting is conveyed in the barest formulas. It is part of the Homeric shorthand not to visualize displacements, and we would often do well not to ask how a character got where he is. Even the descents from Olympus are disappointingly schematic (v. 749–86; VIII. 41–52; XIII. 17–31; XIV. 224–28; XVIII. 616–17; XIX. 350–51; XX. 31–40; XXIV. 77–82, 121–22, 160), and the formula βῆ δ' ἰέναι / βὰν δ' ἴμεναι is as adequate for an immeasurable distance (XX. 32) as it is for a short trip within the camp (IV. 199). The end of a journey is signaled by a colorless phrase indicating that the arriving person stands near, or next to, or in front of, or behind another standing person, or at the head of a recumbent person.[18] At most a conversation is formalized by placing two persons directly across from one another (I. 533–35, III. 424–25, V. 497, IX. 182–96, XXIV. 596–98). The scene of such a conversation is almost totally neglected, a practice that can lead to some curious instances of insulated conversation equivalent to the insulated battle action described above. Thus, in III. 383–420 Helen sits on a tower closely surrounded by Trojan women when Aphrodite appears to summon her to Paris' chamber.

16 Bassett, *The Poetry of Homer*, p. 94.   17 Ibid., p. 50.

18 E.g., II. 20, 59, 172, 197, 790; IV. 92; VI. 75; VII. 46; XV. 649; XVI. 2, 114, 404, 537, 715; XVII. 10–11, 338, 347, 468; XVIII. 16, 70, 169, 381; XIX. 6; XX. 330; XXI. 285; XXII. 215, 228; XXIV. 87, 169.

Aphrodite is in the likeness of an old wool-carder, a disguise obviously designed to make possible a conversation in the presence of others. Helen penetrates the disguise and Aphrodite drops the pretense almost immediately. Yet the following exchange of protests and rebukes arouses no wonder in the surrounding Trojan women; it is as if they do not exist. Similarly in IV. 89–103 Athena seeks out Pandarus, who is explicitly surrounded by his men (IV. 90–91), and communicates lengthy directions apparently not audible to those standing close by him. Or, in XXIV. 126–40, Thetis is able to comfort and converse with Achilles while his companions are oblivious.

In providing background scenery Homer is almost as careless of objects as of persons. As a rule he mentions only one item to serve as a minimum backdrop for the following conversation, or event, or reverie. The absolute minimum of representation occurs when the item is present only by implication: when Iris comes to summon Helen to the wall, she finds her weaving (III. 121–28), an activity that induces the reader to imagine her sitting before a loom. More generally the item is designated. Thus Helen's brilliant portrait of Odysseus' eloquence gains greatly from the scepter he holds stiffly before speaking (III. 216–20). During her interview with Paris in the same book, she acquires a certain decorum by being seated on a chair (III. 424–25). In the Olympian scene at the outset of Book IV the only objects mentioned are the golden floor and the golden cups, but these are sufficient to convey a sense of opulence. I have already remarked on the bow with which Pandarus takes aim at Menelaus (IV. 105–9), an object that so absorbs the bowman's attention that it also comes to dominate the reader's impression of the scene.

The visualizing item need not always be an artifact; when Hecuba goes into her linen closet to seek out an offering for Athena, the one descriptive detail is the fragrance of the chamber (vi. 288–89). Or the detail may be a gesture. In Paris' house Hector is characterized by his grip on a long, shining spear, Paris is busy with his weapons, and Helen directs the work of her women (vi. 313–24). The detail may be tantamount to a stage property, as in the case of Paris' archery depicted against the background of Ilos' tomb (xi. 369–72). Or, finally, the detail may be an architectural or natural object, as when Hector is pictured pondering by the Scaean Gate (xvi. 712) or Agenor by an oak tree (xxi. 549). This Spartan limitation of scenic resources might be labeled the principle of the single property, although strictly speaking as many as two or three properties may be mentioned. The technique is not properly scenic at all. Like the device of frozen motion, it is closer to being sculptural, providing one feature to do service for many. In making use of the technique, Homer avails himself of the aesthetic rule that a single apt impression may be more vivid than a profusion of competing impressions.

Focusing on a single property is in itself a concentrated technique, but it can be further distilled by going beyond the appearance to detail the origin of the significant property. This type of elaboration might be called the genetic description; it penetrates to the manufacture, the material, and the very substance of the object. Thus, in the quarrel of Book 1 Achilles swears his great oath by the scepter he holds in his hand, and as he swears, he tells how the wand was cut from a stump in the mountains and stripped of foliage, how it will not bloom again, and how it is now carried as a symbol of justice (1. 234–39). The effect of this apparently pointless description is to transfer the whole of Achilles' pent-up rage into the inmost recesses of the innocuous object, charging it with emotion and meaning so that when he casts it on the ground at the end of the speech, the gesture is truly thunderous.

In the scene that depicts Pandarus' wounding of Menelaus, Pandarus' bow focuses our attention. The poet accounts not only for Pandarus' handling of the bow, but also for the origin of the horn from which it is constructed (taken from a goat shot in ambush) and for the skill of the craftsman who fashioned it (IV. 105–11). The effect here is to draw the reader's attention more and more inward to the exclusion of all other potentially distracting features in the scene. The excellence of the material, the quality of the craftsmanship, and the skill of the bowman all converge in our minds at the moment of the shot. Again, Achilles' presence during the embassy undertaken by Ajax, Odysseus, and Phoenix is characterized by the lyre on which he plays (IX. 186–89). Homer describes it not only as rich and elaborate, but as a part of the booty taken at the sack of Eëtion. This is perhaps the most imperfectly visualized scene in the *Iliad* because of the vexatious dual with which Achilles addresses his three visitors,[19] but if we concentrate on the person of Achilles as he sits across from Patroclus and tries to fill his idleness with songs of the "feats of men" performed to a lyre won in battle, the anomaly of his present situation and the depth of his wrath become brilliantly vivid.[20]

The scenery of the *Iliad* is both impressionistic and formalized. Enough is introduced to be suggestive, but not so much as to divert us in any way from the course of

19 Denys L. Page, *History and the Homeric Iliad,* Sather Classical Lectures 31 (Berkeley and Los Angeles: University of California Press, 1959), pp. 297–315; Kirk, *The Songs of Homer,* pp. 217–18; Charles P. Segal, "The Embassy and the Duals of *Iliad* IX, 182–198," *Greek, Roman, and Byzantine Studies,* 9 (1968), 101–14.

20 Wolfgang Schadewaldt, *Von Homers Welt und Werk: Aufsätze und Auslegungen zur homerischen Frage,* 2d ed. (Stuttgart: K. F. Koehler, 1951), p. 65; Hellwig, *Raum und Zeit,* pp. 36–37.

events. The settings have no existence of their own; they are merely intimated so as to mark the idea or emotion underlying a given episode. In other words, Homer's scenic technique is symbolical, not descriptive.

The *Odyssey*

Scenic design in the *Odyssey* differs from Iliadic practice to the extent that the scenic inventory differs. Unlike the static *Iliad*, the *Odyssey* embraces a wide range of settings, and in contrast to the open-air battlefield action of the *Iliad*, the *Odyssey* is more often confined within doors, whether the scene is palace, hall, hut, or cave. Subject to these differences, scenic techniques and emphases are similar. There are the same spatial anomalies, the same indifference to scenery as such, and the same isolation of the human component.

Although the *Odyssey* has gone down in literary history as the prototypical story of exotic adventure, the rich opportunities for varied color and description afforded by frequent changes in location are only partially realized. The travel sequences are summarized in barest outline. When Telemachus departs for Pylos, the poet lingers for a few lines over the hoisting of the sail and the rigging of the ship (2. 422–30), but one line suffices for the actual voyage (2. 434):

> All night long and into the dawn the ship pursued her course.

One might argue that this night passage precluded any deployment of scenery, but we will see in the next chapter what extraordinary scenic effects Virgil could elicit from a night voyage. Nor does the visibility improve in the bright light of dawn. The same thrift characterizes the con-

tinuation of the journey to Sparta (3. 484–4. 2), where
Menelaus is able to recount his voyage to Egypt in just
three lines (4. 580–82; cf. 14. 257–58). No less swift are the
legs of the journey Odysseus recites to the Phaeacians, for
example the voyage to the Laestrygonians (10. 80–81) or to
the Island of Helios (12. 260–63) once Scylla and Charybdis
are negotiated. There is no dwelling on sky, sea, or coastline during these stages.

⎮The fullest stretch and the one that best rewards close
inspection is Odysseus' raft voyage to Scheria. For seventeen days he navigates by the constellations (5. 272–78) and
"on the eighteenth there appeared the shadowy mountains
of the land of the Phaeacians" (5. 279–80). The description
emphasizes his navigational skills, not the experience of
seventeen days at sea. Then a storm intervenes, and
Odysseus does not catch sight of land again until two days
and one hundred and twelve verses later.⎮At this juncture
the focus, as so often in the *Iliad,* is not on the view, but on
the beholder. Odysseus' vantage point is atop a great wave,
but his state of mind, not the picture before him, is revealed in the form of a simile: his relief is compared to
that of a child whose father has been released from sickness
(5. 394–97). Only then is the view defined briefly as "land
and woods" (5. 398). As Odysseus swims nearer, the nature
of the coastline becomes more apparent (5. 401–5): reefs,
projecting spits, and cliffs. This is an immediate impression, not surveyed from a distance, but conveyed only when
Odysseus is within earshot and suddenly surrounded by the
roar of the surf. The point is not the panorama, but
Odysseus' alarm.

As he skirts the coast in search of a safe landing, he
comes upon the mouth of a river (5. 441–44). Here he is
finally able to reach shore, but again the shape of the shore

is immaterial; its chief quality, as Odysseus prays to it in deified form, is that it is "much-implored" (5. 445). After the landing, our first view is of Odysseus overwhelmed in body and spirit as he lies on the shore (5. 453–57). The wooded hillside behind him comes into view only when he begins to consider how he should spend the night. Again, the point of the woods is not scenic, but threateningly real: Odysseus fears that he will become the prey of wild beasts (5. 470–73). Throughout this sequence Odysseus himself is the center of attention; his surroundings are important only to the extent that they highlight his skill, his stamina, his fear, and his will to survive.

Once Odysseus is ashore, we discover that overland hikes are no more fully described than sea voyages. Nausicaa's trip to the seashore is blank; there is nothing between touching up the mules and her arrival at the river (6. 81–85). Odysseus' path to Eumaeus' steading is characterized only by woods and hills (14. 1–2). His subsequent trip from the steading to the palace is more interesting because he stops along the way at a public fountain. The stretch from steading to fountain is accounted for in two verses (17. 204–5) and the stretch from fountain to palace in one (17. 255), but the scene at the fountain, in which Odysseus is kicked by the goatherd Melantheus, is more leisurely. The fountain itself is fair-flowing, frequented by the townspeople, built by Ithacus, Neritus, and Polyctor, surrounded by a close circle of black poplars, fed by a cold stream from a rock above, and surmounted by an altar on which wayfarers make sacrifice to the nymphs (17. 206–11). The incidental introduction of this fountain as a setting for the following scene is reminiscent of the landmarks in the *Iliad,* which are mentioned only as they become narratively useful. On the other hand, the details of the Ithacan fountain are more pictorial and more purely ornamental than anything in the *Iliad*.

The fountain is less immediately visual than it might otherwise have been because it is narrated rather than experienced scenery. This is, generally speaking, a feature of the *Odyssey*, which, though richer in landscape than the *Iliad*, fails to absorb the new sense of space through the characters of the epic. Much of the scenery is described as part of a recital, or as a report, or a set of directions, or simply in the form of standing epithets as in the case of "woody Zacynthos" and "rocky Ithaca" (1. 246–47, 16. 123–24, 19. 131). Explicit descriptions are given of the harbor and town of the Phaeacians, Antinous' park, and the interior of his house (6. 262–69, 291–94, 303–10), but they are not a record of fresh impressions, only a summary abstracted by Nausicaa to guide Odysseus on his way. In turn, Odysseus' description of Ithaca (9. 21–27) is a geographical summary for the benefit of his listener Antinous. Similarly, his descriptions of Aeaea (10. 144–52) or the harbors of Helios (12. 316–19) or Phorcys (13. 96–112) are necessarily somewhat faded memories rather than evocative panoramas. On occasion the settings can be completely fictitious, as when Athena, disguised as Mentes, describes the anchorage of her alleged ship (1. 185–86) or when Odysseus, disguised as a beggar, spins his yarn about Crete (19. 338). The fictional settings seem no less authentic than the real ones, a situation which is possible only because description is regularly a feature of retrospective narrative rather than of direct experience.

On the other hand, visual realities can be treated with sovereign negligence. The best illustration is provided by Odysseus' arrival at the house of Antinous. He arrives at Athena's grove outside the city at nightfall (6. 321), a timing which logically ought to inhibit his view. But the poet disregards the sunset in a variety of ways. For one thing, Athena sheds a mist over Odysseus (7. 15), although darkness might have been considered a sufficient guard against premature exposure, and for another, Odysseus is able to penetrate the gloom to enjoy what is for the Homeric epic a uniquely panoramic view (7. 43–45):

> Odysseus gazed in wonder at the harbor and the symmetrical ships
> And the assembly places of the men and the great walls,
> Lofty and studded with palisades, a wonder to behold.

The imponderables do not stop here. As Odysseus approaches Antinous' house, he turns over in his mind the rich variety of the sight before him (7. 82–97; cf. 17. 264–68). Paradoxically, the description includes exterior features he can see, or could see if there were light to see by, and interior features he cannot possibly see whether there is daylight or not. Authorial omniscience has impinged on Odysseus' consciousness and continues to do so through a lush account of Antinous' garden (7. 112–32), including an itemizing of flora which Odysseus can scarcely have picked out of the murk. One wonders how many writers on the *locus amoenus* have noticed that one of the two Homeric examples was observed in darkness. Visibility as such is clearly of no concern; the poet is only interested in the impact that such a scene would be expected to have on the eye and mind of the hero. The imagined response is more important than the actual view.

Among the various visual confusions, those in the Nekyia are notorious. As Bowra summarized: "Since Odysseus is above the earth, there is a real and flagrant contradiction, for it [the Nekyia] presupposes that Odysseus is in Hades

and sees what is there." [21] Not much less troublesome is the
telescoping at the hectic conclusion of the poem.[22]

The *Odyssey* also shares with the *Iliad* an indifference
toward the location of places relative to one another. A
good illustration is provided by the harbors of Ithaca and
Phaeacia. In Book 2 Athena moors her borrowed ship in
the outer reaches of the harbor at Ithaca (2. 391), but there
is no indication of the harbor's position in relation to
Odysseus' house, nor any suggestion of direction or distance when Telemachus makes his way to the ship with the
goddess and his companions (2. 405–6). Only fourteen
books later does it become clear, quite incidentally, that
the harbor is visible from Odysseus' house. Here the suitors
are seated before the gates (16. 344) when Amphinomus observes the presence in the harbor of the ship which has
returned from Antinous' vain attempt to ambush Telemachus (16. 351). Similarly, Eumaeus views the return of
the ship from the vantage point of Hermes' Hill (16. 471),
although we learn nothing about the location of the hill.
In the Phaeacian scene, the arrangement of harbor, city,
and palace remains obscure despite Odysseus' panoramic
surveys in 7. 43–45 and the preparation of a ship in 8.
48–56.

In dealing with the *Iliad* we noted that imperfect attention to scenic detail could result in curiously insulated
combat scenes, lifted out of the surrounding hurly-burly of
the general engagement, or in insulated conversation scenes
that ignore immediate bystanders. Similar moments occur
in the *Odyssey*, though not to the same extent. Since ob-

21 C. M. Bowra, *Homer* (London: Duckworth, 1972), p. 139. See also
Denys Page, *The Homeric Odyssey* (Oxford: Clarendon, 1955), pp. 25–26.
The problem is minimized by Hartmut Erbse, *Beiträge zum Verständnis
der Odyssee*, Untersuchungen zur antiken Literatur und Geschichte 13
(Berlin and New York: Walter de Gruyter, 1972), p. 29.

22 Page, *The Homeric Odyssey*, pp. 112–14. See also Erbse's rejoinder in
Beiträge zum Verständnis der Odyssee, pp. 241–44.

liviousness to surrounding company was a regular feature of the *Iliad,* it is something of a novelty to find in the first book of the *Odyssey* a scene in which Telemachus whispers to Athena "so that the others would not overhear" (1. 157).[23] We may hasten to conclude that this represents a new scenic awareness inasmuch as scenic insulation, to which we have become accustomed, normally would preclude the thought of eavesdropping, especially on a conversation with a goddess. But the new awareness is contradicted later in 4. 70 when Telemachus leans over to whisper his admiration of Menelaus' palace to Peisistratus "so that the others would not overhear." This time the precaution is useless and Menelaus hears quite clearly what is said (4. 76), marking a return to spatial indiscrimination and suggesting that the phrase is merely formulaic.

The poet may on occasion resort to divine intervention in order to resolve scenically impossible situations. The *Odyssey* offers a case analogous to the Iliadic scene in which Zeus obscures the death of Patroclus before the very eyes of Achilles gazing out over the battlefield. When Eurycleia has recognized Odysseus, she signals her emotion first by overturning the bronze basin, which clangs loudly, and then by turning to Penelope to communicate the revelation (19. 469–77). Penelope, who is seated nearby, can hardly fail to notice that something unusual is afoot, but she does not react. The explanation is that "Athena had diverted her mind" (19. 479).

To some extent the *Odyssey* compensates for such imperfections by the use of close-up descriptions in the style of the *Iliad,* but without the constant alternation of focus

---

[23] For the effect of the scene see Friedrich Klingner, "Über die vier ersten Bücher der Odyssee," *Berichte über die Verhandlungen der Sächsischen Akademie der Wissenschaften zu Leipzig,* Philol.-hist. Kl. 96 (1944), I, 27; rpt. in *Studien zur griechischen und römischen Literatur* (Zurich and Stuttgart: Artemis, 1964), p. 57.

toward and away from the details of single combat. Shift
of focus is not a device to provide variety or mobility, as
in the *Iliad,* nor is it needed in this capacity since mobility
is achieved through frequent displacements. The close-up
as a conscious effect is largely restricted to the *Iliad*-like
confrontation between Odysseus and the suitors at the end
of the epic. Perhaps the most brilliant instance in either
epic is the stringing of the bow in 21. 393–423, when all
eyes focus on the unlikely spectacle of a beggar attempting
the test which has defeated all the efforts of the suitors.
The atmosphere is heavy with irony and anticipation as
the soon-to-be-identified avenger inspects and handles the
bow with mock deliberation, allowing it first to dawn on
his spectators that he is not entirely unfamiliar with such
instruments of war, and then stringing it with breathtaking ease. Just as the close description of the scepter
Achilles holds in the quarrel scene transforms it into a
symbol of his wrath, so the dwelling on Odysseus' bow in-
vests it with all the qualities of cunning, prudence, endur-
ance, and strength that go into the act of revenge he is
about to perform. As in the *Iliad,* it is primarily a state of
mind that is illuminated by the description, or rather, two
antithetical states of mind, Odysseus' cool purposefulness
and the folly of the suitors.

The onset of the vengeance is focused in the same way
(22. 8–20). The moment of Antinous' death is frozen as he
is about to drink from a golden tankard "and death was
not in his thoughts." Then the arrow penetrates his throat,
and the picture dissolves as he collapses on the floor amidst
the bread and meat from which he has been feasting. The
moment is distilled to reveal the fundamental characteristics of the protagonists, Odysseus' ruthlessness and the
heedlessness of his victim, who, even at the last instant,
does not see beyond the charm of the banquet.

Other episodes indicate that the poet is less concerned with pictures than with responses. When Odysseus stands naked and briny on the seashore (6. 135–40), his appearance is conveyed not through description, but through the alarm of the maidens, and after his transformation at the hands of Athena, he is visualized chiefly through Nausicaa's admiration (6. 229–45). The pattern repeats itself when the goddess similarily transforms Telemachus (17. 63–64). Natural settings may also serve more as psychological ciphers than as visible realities. Odysseus, longing to return home and escape the charms of Calypso, is pictured as he sits on the seashore gazing out to sea (5. 84, 158); his longing, not the seascape, commands our attention. When he identifies himself at the court of Alcinous, his lingering description of Ithaca (9. 21–27) is not so much for the sake of identification as to communicate his nostalgia and suggest discreetly what aid is necessary for his return to Ithaca.

I noted at the outset that the scenic preconditions of the *Odyssey* differ from those of the *Iliad* in two respects: in the abundant changes of scenery and in a preference for interior settings. The feasting of the suitors, Telemachus' consultations with Nestor and Menelaus, Odysseus' account of his wanderings, his stay with Eumaeus, and his final confrontation with the suitors all take place indoors. Most prominent is, of course, Odysseus' own hall. We have already seen that landscape in the *Odyssey*, though more varied and imaginatively presented than in the *Iliad*, is still visualized in a fragmentary way. The same is true of the interior scenes. This sketchiness emerges clearly from the difficulties encountered by Homerists in reconstructing the shape of Odysseus' house. Debates have centered on such basic matters as whether the house was a one-story or a two-story structure and whether Penelope's chambers faced toward the courtyard or were at the opposite end of

the hall.[24] Where a description of a house is actually provided, it constitutes a catalogue of impressions, not a plan.
Just as the *locus amoenus* passages (5. 59–75, 7. 112–32)
amount to lush but disorganized inventories of vegetation,
so the architectural passages are lists of properties with no
particular arrangement. As Odysseus pauses before the palace of Alcinous, his eyes wander over bronze thresholds
and walls, a silver lintel and silver doorposts, and gold and
silver statuary (7. 82–97). This splendor is calculated to
convey a sense of fairy-tale wealth, not a structural outline.
Similarly, as Telemachus sits in stunned admiration of
Menelaus' hall in Sparta, he whispers to Peisistratus to
mark the gleam of bronze, gold, amber, silver, and ivory
throughout the hall (4. 71–75). The description is only for
effect (4. 74):

> Such perhaps is the hall of Olympian Zeus within.

In the first of these examples the poet depicts the fabulous
wealth of Phaeacia by registering the astonishment of an
onlooker as experienced as the much-traveled Odysseus. In
the second instance, the gawking of Telemachus serves primarily to characterize the limited experience of a young
man who has not yet seen much of the world. In both cases
the description sheds as much light on the viewer as on the
view.

The same is true of a passage in which architectural description is in effect parodied. When Odysseus in beggar's
disguise arrives at his own house with Eumaeus, he breaks
out in a delightfully deceitful paean of praise (17. 264–71).
The object is not to describe a sight already familiar to all
concerned, but only to give scope for Odysseus' continued

[24] Heinrich Drerup, *Griechische Baukunst in geometrischer Zeit*, Ar-
chaeologia Homerica II, O (Gottingen: Vandenhoeck & Ruprecht, 1969),
pp. 128–30, and the literature cited therein.

play-acting before Eumaeus. The pretense goes sufficiently beyond what is necessary to suggest that Odysseus is merely indulging his own guile. It is artfulness for its own sake and illustrates Odysseus' almost wanton cunning, a feature that has jeopardized his reputation, but adds an element of playfulness to alleviate his intolerable mastery of the world and make him more engaging to readers for whom an entirely serious success story is likely to wear thin. Such a scene, in which the hero seems to mock the poet's descriptive prowess by admiring his own house, is one of those welcome glimmerings of the picaresque mode to be found scattered throughout the *Odyssey*.

Generally speaking, interior details emerge only as incidental features of a particular scene. When Athena enters Nausicaa's bedchamber to summon her to the beach, we learn that the chamber is "richly wrought" (6. 15) and that a maiden sleeps by either doorpost (6. 19). When the princess emerges from her chamber in the morning, she finds her mother spinning by the hearth with her maidservants (6. 52–53) and her father about to go to the assembly (6. 53–55). These touches are more compositional than scenic. In the same sequence, Nausicaa gives Odysseus explicit directions on how to find his way into town and into the presence of her parents. She describes the scene (6. 305–9) by saying that he will find her mother sitting by the hearth spinning in the light of the fire as she leans against a pillar, while her father will be seated on a throne, placed against the same pillar, drinking wine like a god. The effect is that of a double portrait. Similarly, when Telemachus returns home leading his father in the guise of a beggar, a good deal of attention is paid to their bathing and entertainment (17. 84–95), but the only visual element is a portrait of Penelope spinning as she sits opposite her son on a

chair leaned against a pillar (17. 96–97). These details have
become formulary and do not go far toward evoking an
impression of the hall.

Where a more general focus prevails, it still falls short
of creating a total scene. Following their efforts to placate
Penelope with gifts, the suitors sit down to pass the evening in feasting, and we are told that the braziers and
torches are lit (18. 307–11), but the poet does not fill in
the picture. We are not told what furnishings or what configuration of feasters is illuminated by the glow. Curiously,
a broader illumination of the scene is suggested only after
the suitors have retired, leaving Telemachus and Odysseus
alone with Athena. At this moment Telemachus exclaims
about a new brightness in the hall (19. 36–40):

> Father, this is a great marvel I behold with my eyes.
> The walls of the hall and the fair ceiling panels
> And the pine beams and pillars, which hold them aloft,
> Shine in my eyes like blazing fire.
> Surely one of the heaven-dwelling gods is within.

This is the only passage in the *Odyssey* in which the outlines of the hall become visible, and we will see below to
what effect Virgil adapts them as a setting for Dido's banquet. But for the moment this brightly revealed interior
does not serve as a setting. It occurs when there is no scene
or action to be set: Odysseus and Telemachus are alone in
an empty room. The sole purpose of the lighting is to an-
nounce the wondrous materialization of a goddess.

The scant detail afforded by Odyssean interiors is related
to the single-property principle characteristic of the *Iliad*
and is just sufficient to provide a minimum backdrop.[25]
The representative detail can be the doorpost next to
which Penelope stations herself (as in 1. 333, 16. 415, 18.

25 Paolo Vivante, *The Homeric Imagination: A Study of Homer's Poetic
Perception of Reality* (Bloomington: Indiana University Press, 1970), p. 17.

209, 21. 64). It can be the pillar against which Demodocus leans (8. 66, 473) or the doorpost by which Nausicaa stands rapt in admiration of Odysseus (8. 458). It can be the doorway in which Athena stands when she appears to Odysseus in Eumaeus' hut (16. 159). It can be the chair occupied by Hermes during his interview with Calypso (5. 86) or the ones occupied by Odysseus when he converses with Calypso (5. 195) and Circe (10. 314). Or it can be the spring at which Odysseus' scouts approach the daughter of Antiphates (10. 107). In each case it is a mere suggestion of the surroundings, an indication locating a speaker without allowing the reader's eye to wander over the scene about him. On the contrary, it tends to fix and immobilize the speaker in the reader's mind.

As in the *Iliad,* the single property is sometimes associated with and emphasized by what I have termed the genetic description. The cases range from great simplicity to considerable complexity. Perhaps the simplest of all is the appearance of Odysseus, still disguised as a beggar, at the door of his house. He is framed by two properties, the ashen threshold on which he sits and the doorpost against which he leans, but only the doorpost is detailed (17. 339–41):

> He sat on the ashen threshold inside the door,
> Leaning against the cypress doorpost, which once a craftsman
> Had skillfully polished and made true to the line.

This passing mention of the construction suggests both the contrast between the clean, solid craftsmanship of the doorpost and Odysseus' rags and, by extension, the thoughts that must be passing through the mind of the man who undoubtedly supervised the construction and now sits huddled as a destitute stranger on his own doorstep. The description gives us a picture of the moment and at the same time guides us into the thoughts of the hero.

Another such scene is the picture of Helen at Sparta surrounded by the properties of housewifery (4. 125–32)—a silver basket with wheels and gilded rims and a golden distaff—gifts, the poet tells us, of the wife of Polybus of Egyptian Thebes. Again, this is not just a picture. The origin of the gifts in Egypt calls to mind the whole Trojan tale of woe and Helen's passionate career, her abduction, the protracted war over her fate, and the vicissitudes of her return. Projecting her quiet domesticity against this turbulent background evokes a mental portrait of her stored experiences and her hard-won tranquillity, and the little glimpse of her story becomes part of the education of the young man Telemachus as he observes her.

The most virtuoso application of the genetic description is the history of Odysseus' scar recounted just as Eurycleia has recognized it (19. 392–466). The effects are multiple. The scene makes use of suspense pitched at an unusual degree of intensity as we read seventy-five lines waiting to see how Eurycleia will react and whether she will betray Odysseus' identity, but the flashback is quite fragmentary, merely suggesting the host of thoughts and memories that crowd into Eurycleia's mind as the sight of the scar sets off a long train of associations. The perspective is, as usual, psychological, not scenic; it evokes the confused realization and the unfused reminiscences nursed over many years and now brought to the surface all at once. Eurycleia becomes "multilayered," to use a word which Auerbach wished to exclude from the discussion of Homer.[26] Her feelings and

26 Here and elsewhere my disagreement with Erich Auerbach's famous chapter on "Odysseus' Scar" will be apparent. It seems to me that precisely in this scene the "background" qualities are more important than the "foreground" qualities. Indeed, the title and drift of my chapter may be understood as a rejoinder to such statements by Auerbach as the fol-

the span of her years spring to life in the poet's retrospective glimpse.

This subject is rich and capable of further elaboration. There are, for example, genetic descriptions of Odysseus' bow in 21. 11–14 and Penelope's storeroom in 21. 43–48, both of which provide special mental insights. The peculiarity of such descriptions in depth is not to reproduce a visible scene, but to intimate a state of mind. The settings remain approximate, but the characters stand out. However, the most concentrated instances of what we may call the inward focus in the Homeric epics are purely descriptive rather than genetic. They belong to the scene of Demodocus' performance (8. 62–70):

> The herald approached leading the excellent bard,
> Whom the Muse loved above all and gave both good and
>   evil.
> For she deprived him of sight, but gave him sweet song.
> For him Pontonous set out a silver chair
> In the midst of the feasters, supported against a great
>   pillar.
> And from a peg he hung the clear-toned lyre
> Above his head, and the herald guided his reach
> With his hands; and beside him he placed a fair table
>   and basket,
> And by it a cup of wine for whenever his spirit should
>   bid him drink.

There is probably more detail here than in the description of any other seating in the *Iliad* or *Odyssey*—a place in

lowing (*Mimesis: The Representation of Reality in Western Literature* [Princeton: Princeton University Press, 1953], pp. 6–7): ". . . but the more original cause must have lain in the basic impulse of the Homeric style: to represent phenomena in a fully externalized form, visible and palpable in all their parts, and completely fixed in their spatial and temporal relations. Nor do psychological processes receive any other treatment: here too nothing must remain hidden and unexpressed. . . . Never is there a form left fragmentary or half-illuminated, never a lacuna, never a gap, never a glimpse of unplumbed depths."

the midst of the feasters, against a pillar, with lyre above
and food and drink alongside. But nowhere is the inten-
tion less scenic. The properties are closely detailed only
because the bard cannot see them. They are therefore
drawn into a tight little circle around him, everything
within reach. And in turn this tight little circle, only as-
certainable by touch, draws us into the mind of the bard
as he listens to the feasting about him, gropes for his objects, and ponders his inner life of song.

We may conclude with a parting glance at Odysseus himself as he listens to the tale of Troy conjured up from the
miraculous resources of the blind bard (8. 83–86):

> These things the illustrious bard sang. But Odysseus,
> Taking his great purple cloak with powerful hands,
> Drew it down over his head and hid his comely face.
> For he was ashamed to shed tears before the Phaeacians.

Here too the portrait is turned inward. We see not Odysseus, but the posture of his emotion. His spirit, once more
crushed by the memory of trials suddenly made real by the
bard, retreats into an invisible space behind his cloak. Both
singer and listener become isolated within themselves, and
the poet succeeds not so much in conveying a picture of
the men as in giving shape to their experience. It is in this
illumination of the inner world more than in any illumination of the outer world that the Homeric epic excels.

CHAPTER 2

Visible Space in
Virgil's *Aeneid*

The literature on Virgil commonly speaks of his pictorial genius and his special appreciation of natural scenery.[1] Critics seem to agree that the title of "landscape-lover" bestowed on him by Tennyson is appropriate, but only recently has Virgil's use of landscape as a backdrop for epic action begun to come into focus with Hans-Dieter Reeker's dissertation on the subject.[2] The present chapter follows Reeker's lead and addresses the ways in which Virgil, unlike Homer, projects his action into a visible scene, which becomes part of the reader's consciousness and contributes new dimensions to the narrative it frames.

Because of the formulaic nature and the episodic structure of the Homeric epics, it seemed best to approach them by isolating general principles that could be illustrated with examples taken more or less evenly throughout the texts. The *Aeneid* requires a different approach. Virgil's sophisticated composition, in which sequence is a nicely

[1] A representative older statement may be found in T. R. Glover, *Virgil*, 2d ed. (London: Methuen, 1912), p. 108, and more recent ones in Alexander G. McKay, *Vergil's Italy* (Bath: Adams and Dart, 1970), pp. 54, 146.

[2] *Die Landschaft in der Aeneis*, Spudasmata 27 (Hildesheim: Georg Olms, 1971). Cf. R. Heinze's negative assessment of Virgil's scenic skills in *Virgils epische Technik*, 3d ed. (Leipzig and Berlin: Teubner, 1915; rpt. Darmstadt: Wissenschaftliche Buchgesellschaft, 1957), pp. 350-54, 397-98.

calculated principle, should be viewed in the order in which it presents itself.

Whereas Homer's Odysseus sets out over the dim sea into an equally dim unknown with only Calypso's instruction to keep Ursa Major on his left (5. 270–77), the hero of the "Odyssean *Aeneid*" sets out on a course made clear to the reader. No sooner is the prologue completed than Virgil proceeds to map the course which Aeneas is fated to follow (1. 12–14):

> Vrbs antiqua fuit (Tyrii tenuere coloni)
> Karthago, Italiam contra Tiberinaque longe
> ostia . . .
>
> (There was an ancient city [settled by Tyrian colonists] named Carthage, far across the water from Italy and the mouth of the Tiber . . .)

Carthage, the intermediate scene, is charted in relation to Italy and the mouth of the Tiber, Aeneas' ultimate goal and the point of his arrival at the beginning of Book 7. We are thus given the geographical limits of the action in the first six books prior to the arrival in Italy, the focal points of Aeneas' experience as he is torn between the Carthaginian temptations and the claims of his Italian mission, and, if we wish to press the allegorical view, a typological perspective on the conflict between Rome and Carthage.[3] Confining ourselves to the scenic aspect, we may say that the stage for the initial action is defined in advance as the expanse of the Tyrrhenian Sea. The boundaries of the scene are Carthage, Italy, and Sicily (1. 34), and the gulf and menace of the waters thus circumscribed are emphasized by such prases as *multum ille et terris iactatus et alto* (1. 3: "much cast about on land and on the deep"), *iactatos*

---

[3] See Viktor Pöschl, *Die Dichtkunst Virgils: Bild und Symbol in der Äneis* (Wiesbaden: Rohrer, 1950), p. 25.

aequore toto (1. 29: "cast about over the length and breadth
of the sea"), and *acti fatis maria omnia circum* (1. 32:
"driven by fate on the seas in every direction"). This is the
stage on which Aeneas is to be presented and which is to
witness his first trial. We know something about the outlines, the nature, and the potential dangers of the scene
before the action begins.

Once the surface is established, Virgil turns to the origin
of the impending threat, Aeolus' cave. Here the scene is
not one of orderly progress as in 1. 34–35 ("they spread
their sails on the deep and plowed up the salt spray with
their prows"), but one of compressed fury (1. 51: *loca feta
furentibus Austris*), strife (1. 53: *luctantis uentos*), and
rebellious energy (1. 55–56: *magno cum murmure montis
circum claustra fremunt*) contained only by Aeolus' lordly
presence as he sits above and regulates the flow. The contrast between the placid picture of ships cutting the waves
and the taut winds straining for release is emphasized by
Juno's words as she appeals to Aeolus. First she refers to the
fleet (1. 67–68):

> gens inimica mihi Tyrrhenum nauigat aequor
> Ilium in Italiam portans uictosque penatis:

> (A people hateful to me sails over the Tyrrhenian Sea,
> bearing Troy and their overthrown gods to Italy.)

The Trojans appear to be on a straight course from Troy
to Italy, realizing their destiny on schedule and without
hindrance. The ease and regularity of their progress is
stressed, with a suggestion of irony on Juno's part, by the
even rhythm and metrical identity of the two lines. But the
picture she has in mind is quite different (1. 69–70):

> incute uim uentis submersasque obrue puppis,
> aut age diuersos et dissice corpora ponto.

(Lend force to the winds, overwhelm and submerge the
ships, scatter them and strew the bodies over the sea.)

Aeolus is invited to destroy the level line by plunging the
ships below it and to break up the direct line by scattering
the bodies of the Trojans across the surface at random. The
regular pattern is to be interrupted and disrupted, and the
reader's eye, aimed toward Italy in the first two verses, is
arrested and cast aimlessly over the wreckage as the straight
line splinters and flattens out.

This conversion of a direct line into disjointed space is
duplicated when Aeolus acquiesces to Juno's request and
releases the winds by jabbing the side of the mountain and
providing a passage for them. They emerge in a straight
line (1. 82: *uelut agmine facto*), but, like a military column
fanning out for the attack, they sweep and eddy to fill the
available space (1. 83: *ruunt et terras turbine perflant*),
then fall on the length and breadth of the sea, stirring it up
from the very depths (1.84: *a sedibus imis*). Giant waves
roll over the surface as far as the shores (1. 86: *et uastos
uoluunt ad litora fluctus*), and the winds seize clouds and
cover the scene with darkness. Virgil manages in this way a
total accounting of space, from the depths of the sea to the
dark roof of the clouds, and from the storm center to the
distant shores, as the waves roll out over the whole surface
of the Tyrrhenian Sea. The space is both deployed and
animated. It is filled with noise (1. 90: *intonuere poli*) and
illumined by bolts of lightning (1. 90: *et crebris micat
ignibus aether*), which have the pictorial effect of riveting
sea and heaven together. The expanse of the scene is
brought to life by thunder, lightning, sudden blackness,
swirling winds, and rolling waves.[4]

[4] On the epic background of the storm see M. P. O. Morford, *The Poet
Lucan: Studies in Rhetorical Epic* (Oxford: Blackwell, 1967), pp. 20–58.

At the center of this awesome tumult Virgil places the Trojan fleet in a single verse (1. 87):

insequitur clamorque uirum stridorque rudentum;

(There ensues a clamor of men and a shrieking of cables.)

The effect of establishing a vast and tempestuous seascape before formally introducing Aeneas into the epic is one of perspective. By magnifying the dimensions of the cosmic assault, the poet reduces Aeneas and his companions to an insignificant speck in the open expanse of sea and sky. When Virgil focuses in on the speck, Aeneas is stretching out his hands into the abyss above him and wishing that he had succumbed at Troy, which his mind has suddenly transformed from a scene of total disaster into a refuge from an even greater misery—to such an extent has Aeolus inverted the natural order. Virgil dwells on the inversion in the great scene of destruction in 1. 102–23, in which he backs off again to a middle distance to observe the onslaught: the wind strikes the sails amain, draws up the waves to the heavens, and opens chasms down to the sands of the sea floor. The ships wallow in the trough, men hang on the peaks of the waves, others are sucked into the void below. The reader has now observed the scene from every angle and level, from a distance in which the fleet can be conceived of as a group of dots and, in reverse, from the foreground perspective of Aeneas' own view, from the shore on which the waves tumble, from the sky on which the clouds gather and the lightning flashes, and even from the sandy depths of the uprooted sea.

The scene began with a transition from calm to commotion and ends with a transition back to calm. Neptune, undisturbed by the upheaval, raises his "placid" head to ob-

serve the scene, and it is as if the elements were already
contained and the tumult quelled by his unmoved and
faintly indifferent gaze. After he gives a bored and patron-
izing reprimand to the unruly winds, the scene is instantly
restored (1. 142–43):

> Sic ait, et dicto citius tumida aequora placat
> collectasque fugat nubes solemque reducit.

> (Thus he spoke, and almost before he had spoken, he
> smoothed the swollen seas, dispelled the gathered clouds,
> and restored the sun.)

Virgil's technique in this opening sequence is not complex, but it differs from Homer's. The natural scenery is
not an incidental feature as in the Homeric epics. It acquires a new priority by being developed beforehand and
in visible detail. We may admire it for its own sake, in a
way we do not admire Homer's storm off Scheria, but we
may also admire the vividness with which it projects the
hero's experience. After the references to Aeneas' sea-tossed
fate in the prologue, the storm serves to visualize and summarize his hardships and to convey an impression of
persistent misfortune, which is absent in the Homeric
counterpart. The increased focus on the elements, person-
alized and magnified as Aeolus and his subject winds,
heightens Aeneas' sense of isolation. He appears to be more
nearly on the brink of spiritual collapse than the indomitable Odysseus on the coast of Scheria, although the latter's
physical exhaustion is more graphically described. The
point is that we must see Aeneas reduced and susceptible
to the temptations of Carthage to a degree never experienced by Odysseus. This effect is achieved by emphasizing
the natural calamities of which he is a victim and the
supernatural malice governing the calamities.

Wearied and weakened, Aeneas now approaches the coast of Africa, and once more Virgil retreats to depict the scene: a harbor protected by an island which serves as a breakwater. Behind this level shoreline is a vertical line marked by two towering peaks rising into the sky. The foreground is the sea, now peaceful and serene. The backdrop (literally: *scaena*) is a rough-textured forest covering the mountain slopes. The scene is particularized by the presence of a cave inhabited by nymphs and made agreeable by fresh springs and stone seats. Up to this point, the view has been toward the harbor, from the vantage point of the approaching ships; only the half of the scenery in front of the viewer has been visible. But after the landing and while his men go about the preparation of food on shore, Aeneas makes his way up one of the slopes and sweeps the empty sea in search of his missing companions, thus filling in the opposite hemicycle and creating once again a spatial totality in the reader's eye, covering the whole area between the open horizon at sea and the closed mountain backdrop.

The primary source for this landscape is the description of the harbor of Phorcys on Ithaca, to which Odysseus is brought by the Phaeacians in 13. 96–112.[5] An important difference in the psychology of the two episodes is that Odysseus is brought ashore sound asleep and is therefore unable to experience Aeneas' immediate sense of release at the sight of a quiet refuge. The waking state not only gives greater scope to the visibility of the scene, but also allows it to impinge directly on the hero's state of mind. A sudden and almost laming deliverance from the torment

[5] On this passage see Gordon Williams, *Tradition and Originality in Roman Poetry* (Oxford: Clarendon, 1968), pp. 637–44, and Reeker, *Die Landschaft in der Aeneis*, pp. 12–40.

of the storm is the next step in the temporary breakdown in Aeneas' sense of mission at Carthage.[6]

Another significant feature of the psychological portrait is Aeneas' seaward gaze. Reeker has pointed out that this motif is taken from the *Odyssey* 10. 97–99 (the land of the Laestrygonians) and 10. 145–50 (Circe's island).[7] But on both these occasions Odysseus' gaze is directed inland in the hope of discovering some human habitation. Virgil might have been expected to imitate this model exactly as Aeneas arrives in an unknown country, the identity and nature of which must be his first concern. Instead, he directs his gaze out to sea, not only providing a fuller view, but enriching the mood of the scene as his eye searches the empty horizon for his lost comrades. The psychological model is not so much the exploratory gaze of Odysseus among the Laestrygonians or on Aeaea as his forlorn gaze into the empty sea from Calypso's island (5. 158). This new collocation of motifs in the *Aeneid* provides a particularly clear glimpse into the mechanics of Virgilian melancholy.

The scene of the landing in Libya is complete in itself, but Virgil assigns it a larger context by placing it within the range of Jupiter's superior vision. As the Trojans rest on the shore and debate the fate of their companions, Jupiter looks down from above (1. 223–26):

> Et iam finis erat, cum Iuppiter aethere summo
> despiciens mare ueliuolum terrasque iacentis
> litoraque et latos populos, sic uertice caeli
> constitit et Libyae defixit lumina regnis.

> (And their meal was completed when Jupiter, looking down from the heavens above on the sail-driving sea,

---

[6] On the emotional content of the scene in general see Pöschl, *Die Dicht-kunst Virgils*, pp. 231–34.

[7] Reeker, *Die Landschaft in der Aeneis*, p. 18.

the sprawling lands, the shores, and the far-flung peoples, paused at the summit of the sky and fixed his eyes on the realm of Libya.)

This is a typically Homeric interlude, but we have noted that Homeric gods glance swiftly. Virgil focuses the scene more deliberately. Jupiter's eye roams over the sail-driving sea, the sprawling lands, the shores, and the far-flung peoples before it comes to rest on the Libyan realm. His eye seems to move inward concentrically over a broad area, the surface qualities of which are emphasized by the adjectives *ueliuolus iacens,* and *latus.* As the focus narrows to Libya, we find ourselves at the scene of the action and of Aeneas' fate, and, in a larger historical sense, at the scene of Rome's fate in the center of an impinging world. Seen through Jupiter's eye, the impending crisis at Carthage has a providential as well as a natural setting.

Olympian interest in Aeneas' fate results in the dispatching of Mercury to induce a hospitable frame of mind in the Carthaginians. At this point our attention is redirected to Aeneas as he sets out with Achates to explore the country and encounters Venus in the guise of a huntress. She announces that the thirteen missing ships with Aeneas' companions aboard have reached harbor safely, and she visualizes the report by pointing out a flock of swans scattered by the descent of an eagle, but now reassembled and safely alighted or about to alight. The augury reproduces the dimensions of the storm (1. 393–96):

> aspice bis senos laetantis agmine cycnos,
> aetheria quos lapsa plaga Iouis ales aperto
> turbabat caelo; nunc terras ordine longo
> aut capere aut captas iam despectare uidentur:

(See yonder twelve swans in joyful formation, which the eagle of Jove, swooping from the aetherial regions, just

now scattered in the open sky; they seem now in orderly
succession about to alight or to look down on the earth
already regained.)

The *agmen* is the orderly formation of the ships before
the storm, the *aetheria plaga* is the surface of the sea, the
eagle plunging from a clear sky is the sudden storm, the
turbatio of the swans is the dispersion of the ships over
the troubled waters; but now they are reassembled in
formation (*ordine longo*) and either in port or in sight of
port. In the metaphor all the main lines of the original picture are reproduced, the level progress of the fleet, the headlong swoop of the storm, and the shattering of the orderly
line across a horizontal plane. Space is fully utilized from
the topmost perspective of Jupiter's eagle, through the
intermediate flight of the swans, down to the earth where
they alight.

With this new reason for rejoicing dramatically im-
printed in his mind, Aeneas proceeds to Carthage enveloped
in Venus' protective cloud. Thus cloaked, he is free to
enter the town directly, as Odysseus enters the town of the
Phaeacians (7. 14–40) or as Jason enters the town of Aeetes
in another model passage from Apollonius' *Argonautica*
(3. 210–14). But Aeneas and Achates stop short on the crest
of a hill overlooking the city and form their impressions
from a distance (1. 418–38). Aeneas is amazed at the huge-
ness (*moles*) of the construction, the gates, the paved streets,
and the commotion (*strepitus*). The inhabitants are busy
raising walls and citadel, laying out building sites, excavat-
ing a harbor, digging theater foundations, and quarrying
vast columns. The whole picture is then summarized in the
familiar bee simile. Thereafter the perspective is contracted. The hill overlooks (*imminet*) the city and Aeneas
has been looking down (*desuper*) on it. But after the simile
we realize that he has approached the city: he exclaims at

the sight of the rising walls and looks up at the battlements (*fastigia suspicit urbis*). A perspective from below has been substituted for the perspective from above and near perspective (Aeneas seems almost to be craning his neck to look up) for a distant perspective.

Like the stormscape, the scene at Carthage is presented to the reader as an elaborate complex of lines and angles. The gates, citadel, columns, and walls form vertical lines, while the streets and construction outlines form intersecting horizontal lines, and the harbor and theater excavations mark a descending line. An impression of fullness is given by the *moles* of the whole enterprise, and the scene is animated by the commotion of the workers and the bee simile, which conveys the milling activity of a construction site observed from a picturesque distance.

There is one important difference between the presentation of the storm scene and the view of Carthage. The former is laid out for the reader by the poet, but the latter unfolds before Aeneas' eyes and is communicated to the reader through his experience of it. The significance of this difference lies in Aeneas' exclamation (1. 437):

> o fortunati, quorum iam moenia surgunt!

> (Oh happy are they for whom walls already rise!)

The scene is not only, or even primarily, pictorial; it is an occasion for the surfacing of Aeneas' longing for his own city and an ironic prelude to his acceptance of this city, so suddenly and attractively revealed to him, as a temporary substitute.

Aeneas, still invisible in his cloud, now approaches Dido's temple with the frieze depicting scenes from the Trojan War (1. 446–93).[8] The frieze elaborates Aeneas'

---

[8] On this scene see Heinze, *Virgils epische Technik*, pp. 322–33.

view of Carthage, but also reveals Carthage's view of
Aeneas. It illustrates Virgil's technique of complementary
perspective, according to which a view is projected first
from one side and then from the other. Just as the Libyan
scene is viewed toward the mountain background and then
away from the mountains as Aeneas turns his gaze out to
sea, so Carthage is first displayed to the Trojans, then Troy
to the Carthaginians. The scene is complicated by a third
mirror, Aeneas' view of the Carthaginian view of himself.
He experiences his own suffering by reflection, as he will
do again when he must tell his story to Dido and experience directly the pity suggested indirectly by the pictures
in the temple. These are two further stages in the disinte-
gration of his resolve in the face of an all too welcome and
strangely paralyzing mood of security and sympathy. At
the same time, as Brooks Otis has described,[9] the preview
in the temple prepares the special bond between Dido and
Aeneas before they meet.[10]

As Aeneas stands before the frieze, Dido approaches surrounded by a crowd of youths. The meeting presents the
poet with a new problem in visible design. How is he to
single out the two important individuals in the crowd and
suggest that they have eyes only for one another? Virgil re-
sorts first to a simile and compares Dido to Diana leading
the dance of her nymphs on the shores of the river Eurotas
or on the ridges of Mount Cynthus on Delos (= *Od.* 6.
101–9). The goddess stands out from the crowd because
she is the leader of the formation and because she literally
towers over her companions (1. 501: *deas supereminet*

---

[9] *Virgil: A Study in Civilized Poetry* (Oxford: Clarendon, 1963), pp. 238–
39.
   [10] The process is well formulated by Karl Büchner, *P. Vergilius Maro:
Der Dichter der Römer* (Stuttgart: Druckenmüller, 1956), col. 323: "In
immer stärkerer Spiegelbildlichkeit neigen sich die Schicksale einander zu,
ehe es zur Begegnung selber kommt."

omnis). In addition, the simile suggests a contrast between a stately center (1. 501: *gradiens*) and a more mobile periphery (1. 500: *hinc atque hinc glomerantur Oreades*), the concentric motion of which emphasizes the center. Clearly all eyes are focused on the leader in the simile and, by extension, Aeneas' eyes will be trained on Dido. Virgil achieves this effect by the use of contrast in motion (a stately center within a moving periphery), a contrast in height which, following Brooks Otis,[11] we may call "supereminence," and, in general, a centripetal design leading the eye inward.

After Dido has received and welcomed Ilioneus and a committee of Aeneas' shipwrecked companions, Aeneas emerges from his cloud, confronting Virgil with a new aspect of the visual problem. Aeneas cannot be set in relief against a group, like Dido, because he stands alone with one companion. Other effects are called for.[12] The cloud suddenly splits (1. 586–87: *repente scindit se nubes*), producing the kind of instant revelation likely to attract attention, and Aeneas is illuminated by a bright light (1. 588: *restitit Aeneas claraque in luce refulsit*). Like Dido, he is godlike in appearance—imbued with "imperial beauty," "the rosy color of youth," and eyes full of "elated charm," just as the hands of the artisan adorn ivory, or as silver or Parian marble are adorned with yellow gold.[13] The portrait is as arresting as the previous one, but opposed

---

[11] *Virgil*, p. 73. On the Homeric resonance of the simile and Milton's use of it (*Paradise Lost* 8. 59–63) see Edward Kennard Rand, *The Magical Art of Virgil* (Cambridge, Mass.: Harvard University Press, 1931), pp. 392–93. On the recasting of the Homeric model see Pöschl, *Die Dichtkunst Virgils*, pp. 99–115.

[12] On the whole passage see Brooks Otis, "The Originality of the Aeneid," *Virgil*, ed. D. R. Dudley (London: Routledge & Kegan Paul, 1969), pp. 27–66 (specifically 50–51).

[13] The effect is captured by Milton in *Paradise Lost* 8. 618–19: ". . . a smile that glowed / Celestial rosy red, love's proper hue."

in technique. Whereas Dido was depicted as the center of a lively group scene, Aeneas appears in sculptural isolation.

The elements in Aeneas' portrait can be fairly well assembled from the *Odyssey*. The sudden revelation is from Odysseus' appearance before Arete (7. 143–45), and the godlike figure, the specification of face and shoulders, and the artisan similes are culled from his appearance before Nausicaa (6. 233–43) and his final appearance before Penelope (23. 159–62). But the drama of the scene and the strikingly contrasted portraits are peculiarly Virgilian, as is the psychology of the situation. While Athena is very much the dea ex machina when she endows Odysseus with special features to impress a series of potentially doubting ladies, the godlike appearance of Aeneas and Dido has a psychological reality absent from Homer. They do indeed strike one another as divine apparitions, as the sequel relates.[14]

The first opportunity for the lovers to observe one another closely comes during the evening banquet which serves as the background for Aeneas' tale of the fall of Troy. It is also Virgil's first opportunity to describe an interior scene and deal with restricted space rather than the extended vistas of open landscape. The scene is set briefly in 1. 725–30:

> fit strepitus tectis uocemque per ampla uolutant
> atria; dependent lychni laquearibus aureis
> incensi et noctem flammis funalia uincunt.
> hic regina grauem gemmis auroque poposcit
> impleuitque mero pateram, quam Belus et omnes
> a Belo soliti; tum facta silentia tectis:

> (There is a din in the hall and voices roll through the spacious room; lighted braziers hang from the golden

---

14 For a negative view of the passage see Glover, *Virgil*, pp. 214–16.

ceiling beams and the torches repress the night with
flames. Here the Queen ordered the bowl to be brought,
heavy with encrusted gems and gold, the bowl which
Belus and all those descended from Belus were wont to
fill, and filled it with wine; then the hall became still.)

The passage, though brief, contains a remarkable variety
of dimensions and textures. It begins with noisy conviviality
(*fit strepitus tectis*) and ends in silence (*facta silentia tectis*).
The noise is centrifugal, encompassing the total scene and
the confusion of voices, but the silence is centripetal and
focuses our attention on Dido in the center as she is about
to speak; our perception of the scene is directed first out
around the hall, then inward. The contrasts between sound
and silence and center and periphery are elaborated by the
description of the sound as a rolling presence throughout
the hall (*uocemque per ampla uolutant atria*), somewhat
reminiscent of Aeolus' winds swelling and pressing outward in their cavernous abode. The hall is filled, and the
contained noise gives us a sense of the ceiling and four
walls as they echo.

The same spatial sense can be observed in the contrast
between darkness and light, visualized by the torches over-
coming night (*noctem flammis funalia uincunt*). We perceive a dark background against which the torches contend,
pressing the night back from the festive center and into the
remoter recesses.[15] At the same time, the lighting suspended from the ceiling outlines the hall. Just as Virgil
joined the extremities of sky and sea with bolts of lightning
in the storm scene, here he joins the echoing ceiling and
the murmuring banqueters with hanging lamps, which
serve to frame as well as to illuminate the picture. Everything in the scene, the enveloping sound and darkness as

15 On the lighting effects in this scene see Pöschl, *Die Dichtkunst Virgils*, p. 272.

well as the central brightness, tends to draw us into the warm and convivial intimacy in which the relationship between Dido and Aeneas is about to blossom.

In addition to the focusing qualities of sound, light, and space, there is a temporal dimension. The votive bowl which Dido raises has been raised before her by her ancestor Belus and all his descendants. The scene Virgil visualizes is thus traditional, stretching back over generations; it has the special sense of continuity and permanence that goes with formal ceremonies. There is a historical as well as a spatial quality of security in the banquet hall. The significance for Aeneas is that Dido has been able to restore a broken tradition after her flight to Carthage, and this is both the appropriate and the ironical background for Aeneas' tale of expatriation and hope as it unfolds in Books 2 and 3.

As Aeneas embarks on his recital, he is brought into sharper focus by another modulation of sound and sight: the dying of the voices from the previous scene, the group turning toward him in anticipation, and his heightened visibility as he occupies a raised couch at the center of the listeners' attention (2. 1–2):

> Conticuere omnes intentique ora tenebant;
> inde toro pater Aeneas sic orsus ab alto:

> (All were silent and looked expectantly toward the high couch from which Father Aeneas began as follows:)

He must now overcome his pleasant sense of inertia, dispel the comforts of the previous scene, and renew his anguished memories: "You bid me, oh Queen, renew unspeakable woe . . . but though the spirit is loath to remember and shrinks from my sorrow, still I shall begin."

At this moment Virgil lifts the perspective to subsume the scene at Troy as well as the scene of the telling: "Already dewy night hastens from the sky and the fading stars entice us to sleep." The vault of the night heavens expands and arches our view, moving the eye effortlessly from Carthage to Troy and back and providing a double background for the night recital in one place and the night action in the other. Once the gliding transition is effected, Virgil's first concern is to establish the parameters of the scene at Troy. Tenedos, where the Greeks have concealed themselves feigning a departure, is located in relation to Troy, and we await the coming developments with our attention focused on the four-mile stretch of water separating the lurking Greeks from the unsuspecting Trojans. We are in effect offered two angles: we may observe the action at Troy from the vantage point of the Greeks or we may adopt the poet's stance above the action because, like the poet and like Aeneas in retrospect, we know what the Trojans do not know. The only angle we are not offered is from the city. Even through the retrospective medium, there is an ominous recreation of the Trojans' unwitting posture; only from their perspective is the scene obscure.

As the action unfolds before the walls of Troy, the Trojans' false sense of release finds expression in a liberation of space: the gates of the city are flung open and the citizens emerge in a holiday mood to wander about the Greek camp and the recent battle sites, to reminisce about fresh memories which already seem remote, and to admire the Trojan Horse. The implied scenic contrast between the serried battalions of a few days earlier and the strolling sightseers who now move carelessly about makes the vulnerability of the open city apparent. The idea of military relaxation derives from Achilles' Myrmidons suddenly re-

lieved of duty in the *Iliad* II. 771–79. In connection with
this scene, we had occasion to remark on Homer's contras-
tive effects, but these effects are heightened by Virgil, who
is dealing not with a phase in the private quarrel between
two Greek chieftains, but with the extinction of Troy.

The debate about what to do with the Trojan Horse is
now engaged, and this imposing and menacing curiosity
becomes the focal point for the next events. Laocoon
rushes headlong down from the citadel with a crowd of
followers (2. 40–41). His sudden appearance narrows and
intensifies the scene, marking out the space from citadel to
shore and drawing the eye in from the crowd of curious
wanderers with the plumb line of his descent and the sharp
note of his exclamations.

At the next moment the scene is further concentrated by
a new line toward the Horse as the shepherds approach
with Sinon, presumably along a path leading from the
open country. The Horse thus becomes the hub of attention, gathering spokes from the city and the country, to
which will be added presently a third spoke along the seaward course from Tenedos. Each spoke reinforces the
destruction of Troy, against which three factors conspire:
the carefree faith of the citizenry who abandon themselves
to rejoicing and fail to heed Laocoon's alarm from the
citadel, the Grecian trickery of Sinon brought in from the
second direction, and, after Sinon's smooth fiction and the
acquiescence of the Trojans, the pronouncement of fate
signaled by the serpents landing from Tenedos and destined
to discredit Laocoon. In this context, the Horse appears
not just as a ruse, but as the center of a converging pattern.
It is not the cause so much as the visible symbol of all the
factors that unite in the downfall of Troy.

The symbolic properties do not detract from the variety
and vividness of the scene. Each of the approaches is alive

with motion and detail. Laocoon rushes in a straight line with his followers presumably trailing behind, unable to keep up either with the speed of his pace or of his thought. Sinon's approach is more deliberately calculated and rich in irony as he is encircled by the contending gibes of his captors, little dreaming that they are the dupes. The approach of the serpents is again different, sudden and sinister. Unlike the scenes dominated by Laocoon's loud exclamations and the exulting of Sinon's captors, this one is silent—except for a ripple of parting waters and the serpentine hissing of Virgil's verse effects. But the silence is counterbalanced by an abundance of visual details: the scene is full of foam, heads raised over a wake of sinuous coils, scarlet crests, bloodshot eyes, and darting tongues. The execution is as swift as the apparition is sudden, and the serpents are no sooner in sight than they are upon Laocoon and his children *agmine certo* (2. 212), in an unswerving and inescapable line. We may observe here how Virgil regulates speed by the way he designs the approach. When a stately or deliberate advance is intended, as in the case of Dido's appearance before Aeneas or Sinon's studied approach, progress is moderated by a thronging circular crowd enclosing and, we may imagine, impeding it. When rapid progress is envisioned, as in the descent of Aeolus' winds on the Trojan fleet or the advance of the serpents from Tenedos, the straight line is unmodified (1. 82: *agmine facto* = 2. 212: *agmine certo*), or the attendant crowd lags behind, as in the case of Laocoon's descent from the citadel.[16]

The scene on the shore assembles the elements and sets the mood for the night action in Troy. The serpents focus the crucial stretch of water from Tenedos and signal the

[16] It seems to me that what Conington writes about 2. 40 does not exclude the sense given by Heyne's reading of the line.

nature of what is to come as they entwine Laocoon.[17] Indeed, the nocturnal attack recreates the spatial and thematic focus of the preceding scene to a considerable extent: the unsuspecting Trojans scattered in sleep (2. 252: *fusi per moenia Teucri*) as they were scattered about the Greek camp during the day, Sinon prosecuting his treachery as he releases the soldiery from the Horse, and the main Greek force emerging from ambush and gliding silently over the waters like the monitory serpents. Night cloaks the deception, but the scene is revealed to the reader by the moonlight which illumines the Greek ships as they approach *tacitae per amica silentia lunae* (2. 255). This is the view from above favored by Virgil in visualizing a general configuration. We are in effect invited to look down on the Greeks as they slip over the dividing sea toward an ill-guarded Troy peopled with men overcome by sleep and wine. Having laid out the scene once already during the preceding day, Virgil now refocuses it so that we may observe the general outlines just prior to the engagement. Then the focus narrows and comes to rest on Aeneas, henceforward the dominant individual in the larger canvas, as he is visited in his sleep by Hector and admonished to flee.

Aroused by the growing din of battle, which ultimately penetrates the protected recesses of Anchises' house, Aeneas mounts to the roof and surveys the desolation below from a middle perspective. The scene is rendered at first through an extended simile describing the natural devastation of a wind-driven fire consuming grain fields or a mountain torrent sweeping them away. But as Aeneas' view sharpens, we see specific houses burn and crumble and the flames

17 See Michael C. J. Putnam, *The Poetry of the Aeneid: Four Studies in Imaginative Unity and Design* (Cambridge, Mass.: Harvard University Press, 1965), p. 25.

reflected in the waters off Troy, and we hear the clamor
of men and trumpets. Virgil's technique is to initiate us
gradually into the scene, which we perceive first as a dream,
then as a dull murmur, then as a sudden and confused
revelation, and finally as a view of itemized destruction.
Only then does Aeneas plunge into the fray, cutting short
our perspective in a realistic way because he and the other
participants in the heat of hand-to-hand fighting have no
overview. The sentries fight blindly (2. 335), the Trojans
advance like wolves made blind by hunger (2. 357), and
black night encircles them with cavernous shadows (2. 360).
The destruction is too vast to be analyzed (2. 361–62):

> quis cladem illius noctis, quis funera fando
> explicet aut possit lacrimis aequare labores?

> (Who can describe with words the destruction of that
> night, or the slaughter, or who can weigh up the suffer-
> ing with tears?)

These verses are an interesting combination of reportorial
dismay and rhetorical pathos, but they do not suggest, as
did Homer's disclaimer in XII. 176, that the poet is unequal
to the situation. They suggest at most that Aeneas himself
could not survey the scene, but that what he did see
registered a profound shock. The blind confusion of the
scene is exemplified by Androgeos, who fails to distinguish
Aeneas' band from his own and falls into their hands, and
by the redoubling of uncertainty that results when Aeneas
and his followers impersonate the Greeks.

In this tangle of fighting there is only one glimpse of
the overall scene as Aeneas and his companions pelt the
Greeks from the roof of Priam's palace after dismantling
"the overhanging tower raised at the topmost point under
the stars, from which all Troy and the ships of the Greeks

and the Achaean camp used to be viewed" (2. 460–62).
This is a startling perspective, unprecedented anywhere in
the *Iliad* and full of exasperating irony as the eye is fixed
one last time on the once-threatening presence just now
thought to have withdrawn and on the Greek camp, in
which the Trojans had disported themselves the same day,
abandoned now not because the Greeks are gone, but because they are in the very heart of the city. This little
glimpse, more a mental association than an actual view,
redeploys for Aeneas the whole ten-year experience and
conveys to the reader what must have struck the Trojan
mind not only as an unexpected, but as a totally irrational
conclusion to the conflict.

When the Greeks break into Priam's hall, we are given
some fleeting perceptions of the action, fleeting, one suspects, because the attack is so sudden that there is no time
for more than a quick impression of a few salient features.
Thus, as Pyrrhus breaks in, the interior of the hall opens
in a long view before him, while those inside, from a
complementary position, see the armed Greeks suspended
for a moment on the threshold (2. 483–85). There is a
clamorous sound of lamentation, the women embrace the
pillars, then everything is swept away in another simile
comparing the scene to a raging river breaking the dikes
and inundating the fields. The embracing of the pillars is
borrowed from Apollonius (4. 26–27—in that instance
doorposts), but the gesture also echoes and contrasts to
the stateliness of a Penelope or the grace of a Nausicaa as
they stand erect and proud beside their pillars in the
Odyssey. Here Homer's poised image disintegrates into a
picture of despairing women clinging to pillars which
themselves are about to collapse. As in Homer, the pillars
function as a single visualizing property, but partly through
Apollonius' example and partly through his own devices

Virgil has enriched their significance as domestic symbols.

After the death of Priam at the hands of Pyrrhus and the realization that all is lost, Aeneas prepares to rescue his family and the household gods from the crumbling city. Anchises, too, though adamant at first, yields to a heavenly token in the form of a falling star. In Virgil's scenic plan the star does double service as a portent and as a spatial contrivance laying out the path for the final sequence in Book 2. It is seen "sinking over the peak of the roof to bury itself brightly in the forest of Ida, marking the way" (2. 695–97). The forest of Ida is the point of embarkation for Aeneas and his followers, and once more we are given an overview as the star arches from Anchises' house to Ida, just as the moon outlined the Greek approach by illuminating the stretch from Tenedos to Troy. The outline is then filled in with the details of the retreat from the city and the loss of Creusa.

In the interest of economy we must survey the remaining books of the *Aeneid* more impressionistically, but the principles of Virgil's spatial design should be clear: the outlining of a scene before it is narrated, the view from alternating distances, visualization through the use of various lines and shapes, animation through sight, sound, and motion, the abundant use of contrast, revelation in the eye of a beholder, and the application of complementary perspective. To this must be added the enriching of almost every scene, beyond the purely pictorial qualities, with emotional and symbolical meanings.

Book 3 covers more ground than any other in the *Aeneid*. The itinerary touches Antandros—Thrace—Delos—Crete —the Strophades—Actium—Buthrotum—Castrum Minervae (Italy)—Etna—Drepanum in a little over seven hundred lines, a breakneck pace compared to the ample narrative of Odysseus' wanderings. But Virgil has a refined

technique for visualizing the legs of Aeneas' journey, as becomes apparent when one compares the plain transitions in
a similar stretch of the *Odyssey* (9. 39–40, 9. 82–84, 9. 105–7,
9. 565–10. 1, 10. 80–81, 10. 133–35). The technique comprises, on the one hand, a system of visual impressions to
convey some sense of variety and, on the other, a formulaic
repetitiveness to evoke the monotony of the voyage.

The framework for each leg is a dual focus on starting
point and destination, but the map thus unfolded is
schematic, providing only a brief mention of either point
and scarcely any elaboration of the distance between them.
The device is essentially the same one we encountered at
the beginning of the poem, where the point of departure
(1. 1–2: *Troia . . . ab oris . . . profugus*) and the ultimate goal (1. 2–3: *Italiam . . . Lauinaque uenit litora*)
are immediately set out so as to establish the total span of
the epic action. On a somewhat reduced scale, the intermediate stage between Sicily (1. 34–35: *Vix e conspectu
Siculae telluris in altum uela dabant*) and Carthage (1.
12–13: *Vrbs antiqua fuit (Tyrii tenuere coloni) Karthago*)
is established in the same way. This summary focus on
departure and destination also obtains in Book 3. In fact,
the first stage of the voyage echoes the span between Sicily
and Carthage, the departure from Antandros (3. 8–11)
being a verbal imitation of the departure from Drepanum
(1. 34–35):

> uix prima inceperat aestas
> et pater Anchises dare fatis uela iubebat,
> litora cum patriae lacrimans portusque relinquo
> et campos ubi Troia fuit. feror exsul in altum . . .

(Hardly had summer begun when Father Anchises ordered the sails to be spread for the destined course and
I departed weeping from the shores and the harbors and

the fields of my native country, where Troy had been.
I am borne an exile over the deep . . .)

The setting of the destination in Thrace (3. 13–14) is
syntactically analogous to the setting of Carthage (1. 12–13):

Terra procul uastis colitur Mauortia campis
(Thraces arant) . . .

(There is a distant country devoted to Mars, a land of
spacious fields, which the Thracians cultivate . . .)

But between departure and arrival there is nothing—the
voyage is summarized with a simple *feror huc* (3. 16). This
is logbook style at its sparest.

The second leg is elaborated ever so slightly, at least in
its first element. After the sepulchral omen issued by
Polydorus, the Trojan departure from the settlement in
Thrace is described as follows (3. 69–72):

Inde ubi prima fides pelago, placataque uenti
dant maria et lenis crepitans uocat Auster in altum,
deducunt socii nauis et litora complent;
prouehimur portu terraeque urbesque recedunt.

(From there, as soon as the sea is safe and the winds
leave tranquil waters and the lightly stirring south wind
bids us set sail, my companions launch the ships and fill
the shore; we are borne away from the harbor, lands
and cities recede.)

The destination this time is Delos (3. 73: *sacra mari colitur
medio gratissima tellus*), but the voyage is again registered
with a simple *huc feror* (3. 78). The echoes persist: *in
altum* = 1. 34 and 3. 11; *colitur . . . tellus* = *terra . . .
colitur* (3. 13); *huc feror* = 3. 16. On the other hand, there
is a visual elaboration in the departure as land and cities

grow perceptibly smaller in the distance behind the exiles
putting out to sea. The slightly sharpened perception is
counterbalanced by yet another echo; the wistful gaze pre-
supposed by a receding shoreline recalls the nostalgia of
Aeneas' tearful departure from the shores and fields of
Troy (3. 10–11).

Once more the Trojans are driven on, this time by an
oracle which Anchises interprets as designating Crete (3.
104):

> Creta Iouis magni medio iacet insula ponto . . .

> (Crete, the island of great Jove, lies in the midst of the
> sea . . .)

Their course takes them through the Cyclades (3. 124–27):

> linquimus Ortygiae portus pelagoque uolamus
> bacchatamque iugis Naxon uiridemque Donusam,
> Olearon niueamque Paron sparsasque per aequor
> Cycladas, et crebris legimus freta concita terris.

> (We leave Ortygia's harbor and fly over the sea, passing
> the bacchanal ridges of Naxos, green Donysa, Olearos,
> snowy Paros, and the Cyclades scattered on the sea, and
> we skim over the waters broken up by many a land.)

The arrival is simply recorded (3. 131): *et tandem antiquis
Curetum adlabimur oris).* In this sequence, therefore, not
the departure or the destination, but the voyage itself is
fleshed out with the sighting of landscape features (mountains, ridges, scattered islands) and colors (green and
white).

On Crete the Trojans are beset by plague and famine
and are redirected once again, this time toward Italy (3.
163–65):

> est locus, Hesperiam Grai cognomine dicunt,
> terra antiqua, potens armis atque ubere glaebae;
> Oenotri coluere uiri . . .

(There is a place, which the Greeks call Hesperia, an ancient land mighty in arms and of fertile soil; it was settled by Oenotrian men . . .)

Familiar syntax and the verb *colere* mark the repetitiveness of the pattern, as does the *uela damus* (3. 191) of the departure, a formula harking back to 3. 9 and 1. 35:

> hanc quoque deserimus sedem paucisque relictis
> uela damus uastumque caua trabe currimus aequor.

(This habitation too we abandon and, leaving only a few behind, set sail and skim over the vast ocean in our hollow vessels.)

On the first leg, the departure from Thrace was brought into special focus. On the second leg, the voyage between Delos and Crete received similar attention. On the third leg, neither departure nor voyage is singled out; nothing is sighted (3. 192–93: *nec iam amplius ullae apparent terrae*), and the passage is obscured by stormy weather (3. 200: *caecis erramus in undis*). Instead, the arrival, this time in the Strophades, is given the benefit of visible delineation (3. 205–8):

> quarto terra die primum se attollere tandem
> uisa, aperire procul montis ac uoluere fumum.
> uela cadunt, remis insurgimus; haud mora, nautae
> adnixi torquent spumas et caerula uerrunt.

(On the fourth day at last a rising land first became visible, mountains were revealed in the distance and curling smoke. The sails are lowered and we lean on the oars; without hesitation the sailors bend to the task, sweeping the blue waters and churning up foam.)

Here the gradual rising of the land (*terra . . . se attollere . . . uisa*) is the counterpart of the receding land in 3. 72 (*terraeque urbesque recedunt*).

In sum, given the narrow confines of a single book and the desire to visualize and characterize each part of the voyage, Virgil chose to emphasize only one phase of each leg, a different phase each time so as to provide both variety and a composite and total impression of sea perspectives. But Virgil must counteract the sense of variety in order to convey the sameness and monotony of a long sea voyage. This he does through a system of verbal echoes, in which each departure, passage, or arrival seems to duplicate a previous one. The landing in the Strophades, for example, is curiously reminiscent of the landing at Carthage in Book 1, with which, one surmises, it may already have begun to merge in Aeneas' mind as he summons up his memories in the retelling. Such a coalescence is suggested by a contradiction in the description of the Strophades: the first view reveals cattle in open fields (3. 220), but in the subsequent view mountains seem to impinge directly on the shore. The Harpies descend from the mountains (3. 225), the Trojans seek refuge in a long recess under an overhanging cliff enclosed by trees and dark shadows (3. 229–30), and Misenus gives his signal from an elevated lookout (3. 239). The landing in Carthage is recalled by the contrast in elevation, the contrast in lighting between the open shore and the dark recesses among the trees, the horizontal line of the coast and the vertical line of the mountains, the curved sweep of the shore, and the illusion of concavity in the cliff rising behind it (cf. also 5. 676–78). The contradiction between open fields and coastal mountains gives rise to the suspicion that the more recent view of the Libyan shore has begun to encroach on Aeneas' recollection of the remoter scene in the Strophades.

The same repetitiveness characterizes the voyage from the Strophades to Actium, the scenery of which recalls the stretch between Delos and Crete. One characteristic feature of each passing island is singled out: wooded Zacynthos (3. 270), the rocky prominence of Neritos (3. 271), the reefs of Ithaca (3. 272–73), and the cloudy mountain peaks of Leucates (3. 274). The first three names are borrowed from the *Odyssey* (chiefly 9. 21–24), where Zacynthos is wooded and Ithaca rocky as a matter of formula. Virgil retrieves the descriptions from their formulaic neutrality. His purpose is not to identify the islands by their standard physical attributes, but to pick out features that would be clear to passing sailors and would tend to fasten in their minds.[18] We are invited to recall that Aeneas, in his account to Dido, is giving the visual high points of a traveler's experiences.

The pattern of verbal monotony continues to build through the remainder of the voyage. The departure from Actium echoes the departures from Antandros and Crete and the arrival at the Strophades: *linquere tum portus* (3. 289) = *portusque relinquo* (3. 10) = *linquimus Ortygiae portus* (3. 124) and *mare et aequora uerrunt* (3. 290) = *spumas et caerula uerrunt* (3. 208). The arrival at Buthrotum echoes the passage through the Cyclades and the arrival at Actium: *litoraque Epiri legimus* (3. 292) = *et crebris legimus freta concita terris* (3. 127) and *et celsam Buthroti accedimus urbem* (3. 293) = *et paruae succedi-*

<hr/>

[18] See Glover, *Virgil*, p. 113, and C.-A. Sainte-Beuve, *Etude sur Virgile suivie d'une étude sur Quintus de Smyrne*, 3d ed., revue et corrigée (Paris, 1878), p. 93: "Tant qu'Enée voyage et raconte ses navigations, on n'a que le profil des rivages, ce qu'il faut pour donner aux horizons la réalité, et la solidité aux fonds des tableaux."

mus urbi (3. 276). The arrival at Ceraunia echoes the departure from Thrace and the arrivals at Delos and Carthage: *prouehimur pelago* (3. 506) = *prouehimur portu* (3. 72) and *sternimur optatae gremio telluris* (3. 509) = *gratissima tellus* (3. 73) = *ac magno telluris amore egressi optata potiuntur Troes harena* (1. 171–72). The landing at Castrum Minervae (3. 530–36) is again reminiscent of the landing at Carthage with its protected harbor, rising pinnacles of rock, and perception of distance in the background (3. 536: *refugitque ab litore templum*).

These fresh Libyan echoes in Aeneas' account not only contribute to the underlying pattern of monotony at sea, but also relate his past experience to the immediate present: Aeneas the narrator at Dido's banquet stays in focus, and we are reminded that his recital has many layers. The epic's retrospective narration gives the story both the visible dimensions of first-hand experience and the mental dimensions of recollection. The two levels of perception are fused by the verbal resonances, which suggest what Aeneas saw on his journey and also how schematic and subject to confusion these distant impressions now are in his mind. We may surmise that the dimness of memory is to some extent self-induced and that Aeneas is all too willing to forget his trials, as he strongly hinted at the outset of his tale (2. 3–13). This sense of repressed and fading hardships prepares us for the return to the present in Book 4, the book of Aeneas' forgetfulness.

Much the liveliest scene in Book 4 is the hunt, more particularly the assembling of the huntsmen (4. 129–59). As the sun rises, the young men pour out of the gates, and nets, snares, spears, hunters, and hounds are gathered in preparation. The scene is variegated and diffuse, full of energy and commotion, a rushing hither and thither, the contending clamor of shouting men, baying dogs, and clat-

tering equipment. Then it is frozen in anticipation of
Dido's appearance (4. 133–35): she lingers in her chamber
as her dignitaries wait on the threshold and her richly
caparisoned charger literally champs the bit. With the
focus on the point at which Dido is about to emerge,
Virgil limits the energy of the larger scene, emphasizing
conscious restraint by picturing the noblemen ready to set
out at any moment and the impatient steed presumably
either tethered or held in rein by a groom. On this ex-
pectant and momentarily suspended scene is imposed the
majesty of Dido's entrance. She advances with a group, but
is separated from them by her brilliance, her Tyrian cloak
with its ornate border, her golden quiver, her hair confined in gold, and her purple robe fastened with gold. This
sculpting technique was used once before to single out
Aeneas in 1. 588–93; it creates an obverse pattern, which
is carried through when Aeneas is described in a simile
previously applied to Dido. In the earlier passage Dido was
compared to Diana guiding the dance of the nymphs on
Delos (1. 498–502); here Aeneas is compared to Apollo in
the same capacity (4. 143–50). Once again the central characters are emphasized for each other's gaze, and the alternation of images and metaphors suggests a blending of
sentiments as they set out on the fateful hunt.

After the storm has arisen to scatter the hunters and
conspire in the nuptials, Rumor is unleashed. As she sets
out, she expands to fill heaven and earth; beginning mod-
estly, she rises into the air, walks on the earth, but raises
her head into the clouds. At night she flies a middle course
between the sky and the earth, and during the day she
occupies roofs and high towers to strike fear into the cities.
Through her offices Iarbas learns of the favor enjoyed by
Aeneas at Carthage and angrily appeals to Jupiter, who responds by dispatching Mercury to urge Aeneas on his way.

Mercury's descent is another exercise in perspective.[19] He first catches sight of the summit of Atlas girt with clouds and pine-clad. Snow covers his shoulders, rivers descend from his chin, and his beard is rigid with ice—a personification which catches the human features of a mountain seen from a distance. The further descent is visualized as a gradually narrowing focus. Mercury, having first observed the facial features of Atlas from afar, settles on the peak for a moment before plunging to sea level like a bird in order finally to alight in Carthage, where Aeneas is engaged in the construction that he had observed from the hill overlooking the city. Acceding to the directives of Jove and withstanding the frenzied appeals of Dido, he makes ready to depart. The preparation of the fleet is described in the Homeric fashion, not directly, but through an elaborate simile depicting the accumulation of grain by ants anticipating the winter (4. 402–7). The simile is reminiscent of the bees used to describe the construction of Carthage, but the visual illusion is greater since ant workers bear a better likeness to human workers.[20] The actual departure is observed by Dido from a lookout over the harbor (4. 586–88):

> regina e speculis ut primam albescere lucem
> uidit et aequatis classem procedere uelis,
> litoraque et uacuos sensit sine remige portus . . .

(When the Queen from her lookout point sees the first light pale and the fleet sailing out before the wind, and perceives the shores and the empty harbor without the sign of a sailor . . .)

[19] Thomas M. Greene, *The Descent from Heaven: A Study in Epic Continuity* (New Haven: Yale University Press, 1963), pp. 74–100.

[20] See Fred Mench, "Film Sense in the *Aeneid*," *Arion*, 8 (1969), 380–97 (specifically 393).

One of the unhappy ironies of the Book is that Aeneas, before whose eyes Carthage revealed itself as a refuge, now sails away before the eyes of the queen he has left with no refuge.

The funeral games organized in memory of Anchises are the principal theme of Book 5. Of the various contests, the boat race is treated most fully.[21] It corresponds to Homer's chariot race in the *Iliad* XXIII. 287–538, but a comparison reveals Virgil's independence of his model especially in the area of scenic design. Homer stages the chariot race in his usual allusive manner. There are no spatial indications prior to Nestor's long-winded advice to Antilochus on the conduct of the race, a silence which seems to presuppose some general knowledge of the course on the reader's part. The advice itself provides no overview, but concentrates entirely on the tiny part of the course represented by the turning post, which is described in abundant detail as a wooden post ("of oak or of fir") flanked by two smooth stones and originally designed as a grave marker for a man long dead. Nestor's strategy concerns only the proper way to turn the post; that is, it singles out the split second in the race when Antilochus' left wheel must almost graze the first stone before making the turn. This is an extreme example of Homer's narrow focus. The only general outlook is provided when Achilles points out the marker to the participants and places an observer by it (XXIII. 358–61). But the orientation of the course does not emerge until we are told quite incidentally that the charioteers started "away from the ships" (XXIII. 365) and that the return leg

21 On boat race and foot race see H. A. Harris' pleasant paper "The Games in *Aeneid* V," *Proceedings of the Virgil Society*, 8 (1968/69), 14–26. Elaborate interpretive comments are put forward by Egil Kraggerud, *Aeneisstudien*, Symbolae Osloenses, Fasc. Supplet. 22 (Oslo, 1968), pp. 118–232.

led "back to the sea" (XXIII. 374). Nor is the entirety of the
race visible to us; for all of Nestor's advice on negotiating
the turning post, nothing is said about this phase of the
contest. Indeed, the onlookers appear to have only a par-
tial view of the proceedings. Idomeneus, who is described
as having the best vantage point, gets up near the end of
the race to look into the distance and give what turns out
to be an inaccurate report on the relative positions of Antilochus and Menelaus. On what happened at the far end of
the course he is able to offer only surmise. Even in judging
the home stretch he is sufficiently uncertain to ask for help,
"for I cannot make it out quite clearly" (XXIII. 469–70).
The final result is in doubt until Antilochus crosses the
finish line ahead of Menelaus by "as much as separates the
horse from the wheel" (XXIII. 517).

Virgil's procedure is altogether different and visualizes
the course in some detail prior to the start.[22] The description begins with the turning post placed on a rock jutting
out of the water offshore (5. 124–25):

> Est procul in pelago saxum spumantia contra
> litora . . .
>
> (There is far off in the sea a rock across from the foam-
> sprayed shore . . .)

Verbally the line echoes *Od.* 3. 293 and functionally it
echoes *Il.* XXIII. 327.[23] But unlike the Homeric usage in

[22] See Heinze, *Virgils epische Technik*, pp. 161–62, and Otis, *Virgil*,
pp. 52–53.
[23] The Odyssean echo is perhaps worth adding on p. 389 of Georg Nico-
laus Knauer's *Die Aeneis und Homer: Studien zur poetischen Technik
Vergils mit Listen der Homerzitate in der Aeneis*, Hypomnemata 7 (Gottingen: Vandenhoeck & Ruprecht, 1964). Although Knauer's book figures
only in this footnote, I have gratefully made use of his listings throughout. In emphasizing the Homeric models for Virgil's line I deviate from
Williams, *Tradition and Originality*, pp. 644–45.

this latter passage, the turning post is not pinpointed as a focus for racing strategy, but widened to provide a general impression of the course. We are told that in stormy weather it is awash in the waves, but in calm weather it emerges as a welcome refuge for sea birds sunning themselves. The description conjures up a general seascape and suggests indirectly that the weather is calm and clear since these are the conditions under which the rock is visible. On the rock Aeneas sets the oaken post (5. 130–31):

> . . . unde reuerti
> scirent et longos ubi circumflectere cursus.

> (. . . whence they would know to return and guide the long sweep of their course.)

Thus, along with the layout of the course from the shore to the rock and back, some sense of the distance is conveyed, no matter how vaguely, by the *longi cursus*. The reader may imagine the course seen from the perspective of the birds already painted into the picture. Then it comes to life with sound and motion as the starter's trumpet blares and the oarsmen shout, digging in their oars and plowing up the surface. As a final touch, Virgil frames the scene by adding the applause and the partisan urging of the onlookers (5. 148–50):

> tum plausu fremituque uirum studiisque fauentum
> consonat omne nemus, uocemque inclusa uolutant
> litora, pulsati colles clamore resultant.

> (The whole grove resounds with the applause and the din and the urging of partisan men, and the enclosed shores echo their voices and the clamor rebounds from the hills.)

These lines evoke both the audience participation and the
natural surroundings, the shore and the tree-covered hills
behind it. As these hills resound with the shouts, their
resonance animates the scene and integrates the action and
the response to it in the kind of reciprocal pattern of ex-
citement characteristic of an athletic contest in a stadium.
Once again, Virgil is concerned with a total representation
of the space against which his action is set and establishes
it in advance. The details of the race and the shifting positions that provide the drama are consistently visible—we
are not allowed to lose track of what happens as we are in
Homer's chariot race. Gyas leads with Cloanthus close behind and Mnestheus and Sergestus vying for third place.
Then at the rock Gyas' helmsman gives too wide a berth
and Cloanthus slips by on the inside to win, while Sergestus runs his ship on the rocks and Gyas, having thrown
his helmsman overboard, steers an uncertain course and
falls behind.

The staging of other contests is less elaborate, for example, the foot race (5. 286–90):

> Hoc pius Aeneas misso certamine tendit
> gramineum in campum, quem collibus undique curuis
> cingebant siluae, mediaque in ualle theatri
> circus erat; quo se multis cum milibus heros
> consessu medium tulit exstructoque resedit.

> (With this contest concluded, faithful Aeneas proceeds
> to a grassy field which woods on curving hills encircled
> on all sides, and in the center of the valley there was an
> arena; thither in the midst of many men the hero went
> and seated himself on a raised stand.)

This scene may be contrasted to the unstaged foot race in
Od. 8. 120–22 (cf. *Il.* XXIII. 757–58):

These then contested first in a foot race.
For them a track was marked out from the starting line
      and
Together they flew, swiftly raising the dust on the plain.

Virgil seems almost instinctively to establish landscape
lines, the flat surface of the grassy field, the wooded hills
in the background, the circular outline of the enclosed valley, and the graded perspective afforded by Aeneas' raised
seat.

The boxing match is managed differently. It bears little
resemblance in detail to the contest in the *Iliad* xxiii. 651–
99, but Virgil nonetheless contrives it with a close imitation of dramatic techniques familiar from Homer, notably
the charged artifact and the genetic description. The ex-
citement is concentrated in Eryx's immense boxing gloves,
which Entellus casts into the center of the scene. All eyes
fasten on them, the brash Dares recoils, and Aeneas turns
them over and over in admiration (5. 400–408). The story
behind the gloves (Eryx wore them when he was defeated
and killed by Hercules) adds to the tension by introducing
an imponderable element of tradition and pride which
Entellus has inherited from his master. In contrast to the
natural theater laid out for the boat race, the mood for the
boxing match is set by a single item, which foreshadows
the outcome of the contest, the victory of Entellus' still
massive strength and determination over Dares' youth and
speed.

The central books, 6, 7, and 8, are not rich in scenic effects, but we may dwell for a moment on two sequences.
Book 7 begins with the final and most haunting passage in
the sea voyage, the stretch between Caieta and the mouth
of the Tiber. It is a night voyage illumined by a bright
moon shedding a tremulous light on the sea below (7. 8–9)

—we seem not yet to have escaped the enchantment of the underworld. As the Trojans pass the island of Circe, the night air is filled with the sound of her incantations and the chorus of her bewitched beasts; for the visible impressions of previous legs of the journey, Virgil substitutes eerie auditory effects on this last one. When the voyagers emerge from the magical night into the rosy light of dawn, the breeze dies, and they must pull their oars in the refractory marble surface of the becalmed waters (7. 27–28).[24] And as they approach the shore, Aeneas beholds the great grove from which the Tiber, yellow with sand, eddies into the sea, and which is animated and made resonant by wheeling birds. This is one of the finest depictions of mood in the poem; [25] it restores Aeneas to reality by imperceptible stages, from the netherworldliness of Book 6, through the irreality of Circe's realm, to the revelation of Latium, from Stygian gloom, through the phosphorescence of a moonlit night, to the bright light of a new day, from shimmering reflections, through the still, marblelike surface of the morning, to the immediacy of the yellow and realistically turbulent waters of the Tiber. Considering that Virgil allows only thirty-two verses between Aeneas' return from the underworld and his arrival at the Tiber, the transition seems abrupt. But it takes place in such a trancelike atmosphere that epic time seems suspended and we shed outer reality to enter Aeneas' mind as it lingers at first in the underworld experience, then emerges by degrees into the new wonder of his arrival at his predestined home in Italy. His sense of time becomes our sense of time,

24 On this passage see Reeker, *Die Landschaft in der Aeneis*, pp. 58–62, 74.

25 Friedrich Klingner, *Virgil: Bucolica, Georgica, Aeneis* (Zurich and Stuttgart: Artemis, 1967), p. 498. Klingner speaks of the "ungemeine Zauber der Vorstellungen und Klänge" on the occasion of this "unbewusste Ankunft in Latium."

and his perception is drawn out by the magnitude of the last transition.

The same magical quality attaches to Aeneas' trip up the Tiber in Book 8 in quest of Evander's allegiance. We could argue an analogy; as the dreamlike voyage in Book 7 returns Aeneas from the underworld to the real world, so the magical trip of Book 8 divests him again of his ordinary existence as he regresses into the penumbra of mythical Arcadian Rome. There is something of the time machine about these journeys. In the latter instance, the supernatural associations begin with the appearance of Father Tiber, directing Aeneas in his way and promising to facilitate his passage upstream.[26] The description of the passage 8. 86–101) is brief but suggestive: Tiber arrests the current during the night, smoothes out the surface, and makes it still—the only sound as Aeneas sets out is the lapping of the water on the gliding vessel.[27] The progress of the ships bemuses nature (8. 91–93):

> . . . mirantur et undae,
> miratur nemus insuetum fulgentia longe
> scuta uirum fluuio pictasque innare carinas.

> (. . . the waves marvel and the grove marvels at the unwonted sight of the shields of men flashing in the distance and painted ships gliding on the river.)

The rhythm of the trip is conveyed by the monotonous succession of bends and the overhanging vegetation, which forms a continuous roof of changing plant life (8. 95–96):

> et longos superant flexus, uariisque teguntur
> arboribus, uiridisque secant placido aequore siluas.

[26] On this passage in general see Heinze, *Virgils epische Technik*, pp. 364–65.

[27] I cannot believe that commentators such as Conington, Page, and MacKail are right in interpreting *rumore secundo* as a shout from the

> (And they surmount the long bends covered by various
> trees, and they cleave the green woods on quiet waters.)

The scene acquires its enchantment from a sense of suspended animation and from a special proximity between
men and nature.

At noon the next day the men catch sight of the walls,
citadel, and scattered houses of Pallanteum, and they make
for the city, before which the Arcadians are celebrating a
feast in honor of Hercules. A residue of the night's mystery
clings to the ships as they come into view and startle the
Arcadians (8. 107–10):

> ut celsas uidere rates atque inter opacum
> adlabi nemus et tacitos incumbere remis,
> terrentur uisu subito cunctique relictis
> consurgunt mensis.

> (When they saw the high vessels gliding toward them
> through the dense trees and the silent men leaning on
> their oars, they were affrighted by the sudden apparition
> and all arose at once and abandoned the tables.)

But Pallas rushes up and calls out to the newcomers *procul
e tumulo,* breaking the spell and restoring normal con-
tacts. The "time machine" has wound down, and we are
back on firm ground, where the natural spatial perceptions
of distance, elevation, and visibility prevail.

Equally expressive is the departure from Pallanteum
after the alliance is contracted (8. 585–96). Aeneas leads
the column, in which Pallas is centered conspicuously, like
the morning star, and they pick their way over the scrubby
ground toward the grove of Silvanus. The apprehensive
Arcadian mothers watch from the walls as the bright

---

crew, and I fall back on Heyne and Henry. It would be a travesty to
break the stillness of the scene with a lusty shout.

panoply recedes in the dust stirred up by the tramping steeds—a vivid perspective and a vivid anticipation of Pallas' fate.[28]

Passing on quickly to the final battle books, we may begin with the simple observation that Virgil strives, with some success, to surpass Homer in the surveyability of his battle scenes. He accomplishes this through a heightened consciousness of the natural surroundings, a sense of spacing, and the utilization of the onlooker's viewpoint.[29] We may illustrate the operation of these principles from Book 10, where, unlike the relatively simple siege action of Book 9 and the two-sided conflict in the *Iliad*, there is a many-sided encounter. Virgil is able to give some account of Ascanius in the camp invested by Turnus' Rutulians and Latins, of Turnus' Etruscan ally Mezentius and his son Lausus, of Aeneas' arrival by ship with his Etruscan allies, of Pallas' arrival overland with the Arcadian cavalry, and then of the general engagement in which all these forces are variously involved. The scene is complicated and requires a sophisticated discrimination of space and action in order not to become blurred. How does Virgil maintain visibility?

As Aeneas arrives with his fleet, he is doubly conspicuous (10. 260–62):

> Iamque in conspectu Teucros habet et sua castra
> stans celsa in puppi, clipeum cum deinde sinistra
> extulit ardentem.

> (And standing in the high stern he already had the Trojans and his camp in view when he held up his blazing shield in his left hand.)

---

[28] On the departure see Pöschl, *Die Dichtkunst Virgils*, p. 278.

[29] On the difference in spirit and viewpoint between Homeric and Virgilian battle action see Glover, *Virgil*, pp. 49–51.

He stands on the high stern so that he is in prominent view and he emphasizes his visibility by raising his gleaming shield of divine manufacture for all to see. We should associate the scene with Achilles' appearance on the trench in the *Iliad* xviii. 202–29, characterized by a divine fire flashing from his head, but it will be recalled that on this occasion Achilles draws attention to himself with his shout. For Virgil the visual impression is primary and Aeneas' posture is immediately apparent to his besieged Trojans, who take heart and redouble their efforts (10. 262–63):

> clamorem ad sidera tollunt
> Dardanidae e muris, spes addita suscitat iras . . .

> (From the walls the Trojans raise their shouts to the heavens and the addition of hope rouses their fury . . .)

At the same time, Turnus and his chieftains look back to discover what has happened, and Aeneas' Achillean appearance becomes explicit with the description of his blazing helmet (10. 267–71):

> at Rutulo regi ducibusque ea mira uideri
> Ausoniis, donec uersas ad litora puppis
> respiciunt totumque adlabi classibus aequor.
> ardet apex capiti cristisque a uertice flamma
> funditur et uastos umbo uomit aureus ignis:

> (But the Rutulian king and the Italian chieftains marveled, until they looked back at the ships headed for shore and the whole sea afloat with vessels. The crown of his head was ablaze and a flame shot out from the summit of his crest and his golden shield emitted fire:)

These lines afford an overall view of defenders first sighting relief from the superior vantage point of their camp walls and intensifying the struggle while, a little late, the

Rutulians and Latins turn about to find Aeneas closing in from behind. This is a strategic viewpoint, unfamiliar from Homer, and Turnus responds to it in strategic terms, dividing his forces and assigning one contingent to the landing troops while they are still in the shallows and have not gained a firm footing (10. 276–84, 308–9), but maintaining the siege with a second contingent (10. 285–86). The difficulty of the landing is visualized by what happens to Aeneas' ally Tarchon, whose ship, despite his careful maneuvering, disintegrates beneath him as it is caught on a shoal. A stubborn struggle then ensues on the beach; both the scenery and the historical import of the action are summed up in the phrase *certatur limine in ipso Ausoniae* (10. 355–56: "they struggle on the very threshold of Italy"). The description itself contains some monumentally unyielding battle lines (10. 358–61):

> non ipsi inter se, non nubila, non mare cedit;
> anceps pugna diu, stant obnixa omnia contra:
> haud aliter Troianae acies aciesque Latinae
> concurrunt, haeret pede pes densusque uiro uir.

> (They cede not to each other, as the clouds cede not to the sea, nor the sea to the clouds; the encounter long remains blunted and the masses stand straining together: thus did the Trojan lines and the lines of the Latins collide, foot was fixed against foot and man was pressed against man.)

At this point Virgil's scenic control falters as we turn to another part of the battlefield where the Arcadians are for the moment giving ground before the Latins (10. 362–65), although Virgil, quite against his custom, has in no way initiated us into the scene for this phase of the action.[30]

[30] Most commentators take no notice of this anomaly, but Heyne (to 10. 362) saw the need to justify the slightly elliptical account: "Arcades,

As if to compensate for this omission, he specifies the landscape; the Arcadians have been forced to dismount because of the rough, rock-strewn gully in which they are
fighting. Here as on the shore we have a clear impression
of the terrain such as Homer never provides. The picture
then dissolves into a sequence of fighting comprising the
aristeia of Pallas, his single combat with and death at the
hands of Turnus, Aeneas' aristeia, Turnus' pursuit of a
phantom Aeneas, more general fighting around Mezentius,
and finally Aeneas' slaying of Lausus and Mezentius, all
in the regular alternation of general mêlée and single combat which is Virgil's as well as Homer's guiding principle
in articulating the battle books.

When the fighting resumes before the city of Latinus in
Book 11, after Turnus has frustrated Latinus' bid for
peace and gone off to waylay Aeneas in a defile, Camilla
leads a detachment of Latins against a force of Trojans
and Etruscans. Virgil's concern here is not with the terrain, a description of which would be cumbersome in view
of the landscape detail just lavished on Turnus' ambush
(11. 522–31), but with the manner in which battle is
joined (11. 597–615):

> At manus interea muris Troiana propinquat,
> Etruscique duces equitumque exercitus omnis
> compositi numero in turmas. fremit aequore toto
> insultans sonipes et pressis pugnat habenis
> huc conuersus et huc; tum late ferreus hastis
> horret ager campique armis sublimibus ardent.
> nec non Messapus contra celeresque Latini
> et cum fratre Coras et uirginis ala Camillae

equites ex Pallanteo ducti et a Pallante praemissi (v. sup. 238. 239), alia
ex parte Rutulos adorti erant (nec opus erat, ut poeta commemoraret,
quomodo Tiberim traiecissent) et duce Pallante pugnabant ea parte lit-
toris, qua torrens in mare exierat; . . ."

aduersi campo apparent, hastasque reductis
protendunt longe dextris et spicula uibrant,
aduentusque uirum fremitusque ardescit equorum.
iamque intra iactum teli progressus uterque
substiterat: subito erumpunt clamore furentisque
exhortantur equos, fundunt simul undique tela
crebra niuis ritu, caelumque obtexitur umbra.
continuo aduersis Tyrrhenus et acer Aconteus
conixi incurrunt hastis primique ruinam
dant sonitu ingenti perfractaque quadripedantum
pectora pectoribus rumpunt;

But in the meantime the band of Trojans approaches
the walls, and the Etruscan chieftains and all the cavalry detachments were deployed in formation. The plain
resounds and the exulting steeds strain at their reins,
wheeling hither and thither; then the field of iron bris-
tles far and wide with spears and the plain is ablaze
with arms raised aloft. Messapus and the swift Latins,
and Coras with his brother, and the wing under the
maiden Camilla appear across the field and they thrust
their pikes with arms drawn back and brandish their
spears; the advance of men and the pounding of horses
wax on the air. Each line halted when it had advanced
to within spear-range; then they burst out in a sudden
shout and urge on their furious steeds; they pour forth
simultaneously a host of spears from every direction,
like a blizzard, and the sky is obscured by the shadow.
At once Tyrrhenus and bold Aconteus run together
bracing opposing spears, the first to wreak loud destruction, and they clash their mounts against each other,
crushed breast against breast.)

The picture is articulated in some detail. An idea of military organization is supplied by the division of the Trojan-
Etruscan force into squadrons (599) and the mention of

Camilla's "wing" (604). Sound is provided by the tramping of the horses (599–600), the shouting (609–10), and the din of the shock (614). Light and texture are supplied by the bristling fields (601–2), the shining arms (602), and the shadowing missiles (610–11), martial ardor by the horses impatient of their reins (600), the brandishing of arms (605–6), the "blazing" eagerness of men and horses (607), and the exhortation of the horses by their riders (610). The structure of the scene builds from the marshaling of troops, to a general view of the gleam and bristling of the battle lines, the advance with poised spears, the exchange of missiles from a distance, and finally the shock of the cavalry as the troops actually collide.

The measured effect of the passage may be compared to the first clash between Greeks and Trojans at the beginning of Book III in the *Iliad*. The Homeric account, with its mighty similes and the clamorous advance of the Trojans against the ominous silence of the Greeks, is undoubtedly more powerful, but the passage is characteristically Homeric in its impressionism. The mass movements are visualized only in similes and thereafter our attention is immediately drawn in on two individuals, Paris and Menelaus. We cannot be certain whether the engagement has begun in some minor way before the action is arrested to allow for the single combat between the two opposing warriors. In this area of intermediate visibility Virgil intervenes; what he cannot achieve in sweep and grandeur, he compensates for with a greater refinement in detail.

One other scenic mutation of the Homeric model in Book 11 is indicative of Virgil's technique. After the death of Camilla, the nymph Opis descends to the battlefield to execute Diana's vengeance on Arruns. The sequence is modeled closely on Pandarus' shot in the *Iliad* IV. 89–149,

a moment set against the background of Ilos' tomb. Virgil
borrows the tomb for Opis' shot (11. 849–53):

> fuit ingens monte sub alto
> regis Dercenni terreno ex aggere bustum
> antiqui Laurentis opacaque ilice tectum;
> hic dea se primum rapido pulcherrima nisu
> sistit et Arruntem tumulo speculatur ab alto.

(Under the soaring mountain there was a great barrow
of earth for the ancient king of the Laurentians Dercennus, covered with dense ilex; here the fair goddess
first settled from her swift flight and observed Arruns
from the high mound.)

Here, as in the *Iliad,* the tomb is unexplained. It has not
been mentioned before, and nothing is known of Dercennus. But, whereas the sudden presence of a tomb was
disturbing in the midst of the perfectly natural action on
the Trojan plain, these slightly mysterious qualities are
precisely what make the tomb of Dercennus appropriate
for Opis' shot. She is herself a mysterious presence, unseen and quasi-symbolical. It is proper that her location
should be unclear. At the same time, Virgil's sense of
scenery leads him to place the mound at the foot of a commanding mountain and to adorn it, not with the bare
shaft of a column, as Homer did, but with a natural
growth of ilex.

While Books 10 and 11 illustrate Virgil's control of the
general battlefield, Book 12 is preoccupied with the momentous encounter between Aeneas and Turnus, which is
the chief specimen of the single combat. It is a finer book
than the two preceding and exemplifies one last time the
poet's ability to extract emotional riches from the struc-
turing of his scenes. The stage is set with deliberation and
a certain portentousness: the combat for final possession of

the city is to take place beneath its walls, and even the
tired dawn formula is arresting because it marks the last
sunrise of the poem (12. 113–19): [31]

> Postera uix summos spargebat lumine montis
> orta dies, cum primum alto se gurgite tollunt
> Solis equi lucemque elatis naribus efflant:
> campum ad certamen magnae sub moenibus urbis
> dimensi Rutulique uiri Teucrique parabant
> in medioque focos et dis communibus aras
> gramineas.

> (Then the day just dawning scattered the tops of the
> mountains with light as the sun's horses rise from the
> deep and breathe forth light from nostrils held high.
> The Rutulians and Trojans measured out a field for the
> battle under the walls of the great city and prepared in
> the center hearths and grassy altars for their common
> gods.)

The Latin host emerges from the city, and the Trojan and
Etruscan forces gather opposite, their leaders resplendent
in gold and purple. All are variously armed, but at a given
sign the spears are fixed in the earth and the shields leaned
against them. Above the scene the spectators assemble, the
mothers, the noncombatants, and the old men, filling
rooftops, towers, and the platforms above the gates. From
an even higher vantage point Juno looks on from the
Alban Mount. But this is a false portentousness because
Turnus' immortal sister Juturna, with Juno's sanction, is
able to stir up the Latins and disrupt the solemn preparations with another outbreak of general fighting. Only
toward the end of the book and in the face of a city already
in flames does Turnus finally disdain his sister's intervention and turn to meet Aeneas alone. Now with the focus

---

[31] See Heinze, *Virgils epische Technik*, pp. 321–22.

turned inward on Turnus' resignation and outward on
Aeneas' indomitable stature (tall as Athos or Eryx or
Father Apennine), the champions advance on one another.
Once again all eyes are turned on them (12. 704–9):

> iam uero et Rutuli certatim et Troes et omnes
> conuertere oculos Itali, quique alta tenebant
> moenia quique imos pulsabant ariete muros,
> armaque deposuere umeris. stupet ipse Latinus
> ingentis, genitos diuersis partibus orbis,
> inter se coiisse uiros et cernere ferro.

(Then indeed did the Rutulians and the Trojans and
all the Italians turn their eyes in emulous unison, those
who occupied the high walls and those who were batter-
ing the walls below with a ram, and they stripped their
arms from their shoulders. Latinus himself is amazed to
see the two huge men, born far apart on the earth, coming together to decide the issue with steel.)

From the moment of the first impact the eyes remain fixed,
as we are reminded by the comparison of the onlookers to
cattle struck dumb by fear at the sight of two bulls colliding in battle over the leadership of the herd (12. 718–19).
Then Jupiter weighs the balance of fate and Turnus'
sword breaks, leaving him to be pursued at will before the
city. The reader will recall how spatially unclear the pursuit of Hector is in the *Iliad* xxii. 145–66. The description
leaves open the question of why Hector cannot after all
escape, but must continue in circles.[32] No such question
arises in the *Aeneid;* Turnus is hemmed in by the Trojan
bystanders, a swamp, and the walls (12. 744–45). He calls
out to the Rutulians asking for his sword, for which he
had mistakenly substituted the one now broken, but

[32] See Samuel E. Bassett, *The Poetry of Homer,* Sather Classical Lectures 15 (Berkeley: University of California Press, 1938), p. 51.

Aeneas discourages any such aid with threats of instant death. The filling in of the surroundings and the charged and desperate words which pass between the combatants and the onlookers integrate the scene. Virgil binds the onlookers to Turnus' fate, and the effect is heightened by the role of Juturna, who first restores her brother's sword and then, perceiving the Dira sent against him by Jupiter, must finally abandon him in bitterness and sorrow. Turnus is more immediately a center of tribal and familial grief than Hector.[33] Nor is the concern unilateral; Turnus, too, sweeps a parting look over what he is about to leave (12. 915–18): [34]

> Rutulos aspectat et urbem
> cunctaturque metu letumque instare tremescit,
> nec quo se eripiat, nec qua ui tendat in hostem,
> nec currus usquam uidet aurigamue sororem.

(He looks at the Rutulians and the city, he pauses in fear and trembles to face death, but he sees no way to escape, nor does he know what will avail against his enemy, and nowhere does he perceive his chariot or his charioteering sister.)

The pain of parting and the pain of abandonment merge in these lines, which show Turnus alone between friend and foe. His solitary end is all the more obvious for being placed in intimate surroundings, and his time ebbs out with a fullness and an awareness on his part not paralleled in the deaths of Homeric heroes. In the course of the book he has grown into a knowledge of his fate through the experience of fear, the humbling reliance on his sister, the

33 Pöschl, *Die Dichtkunst Virgils*, p. 217: "Der Kampf selbst ist erhöht von der Resonanz der Zuschauerschaft, ja der ganzen Natur, während um Hektors Tod beängstigende Leere herrscht."

34 This touch was imitated by Voltaire (*Henriade* 10. 160) in describing the death of d'Aumale: "Il regarde Paris, et meurt en soupirant."

failure of weapons and flight, and his helplessness before
the unremitting Aeneas. Each scene is a supplementary
revelation and contributes to the growing recognition of
doom. Much of the effectiveness of the final book lies in
the manner in which the successive scenes visualize the
severing of Turnus from those about him and his emer-
gence into a new consciousness and a new self-reliance. It
is characteristic of Virgil at his best that he makes his
scenes not only pictorial, but also psychologically trans-
parent. The pictorial qualities were imitated, albeit imperfectly, by later epic writers, but the transparency was
never recaptured.

Spatial Design in the Carolingian Epic

Among the renascence phenomena inspired under the reign of Charlemagne and persisting through the reign of his son Louis the Pious was a renewal of the ancient epic form. The resulting texts never attain dimensions that would allow us to refer to them as true epics, but they have a certain interest as the first medieval attempt to recapture the Roman epic manner. Of the available models, Virgil's *Aeneid* took precedence. Carolingian writers were steeped in Virgil, and the reader is arrested by Virgilian lines and phrases at every turn, but the question to be pursued here is whether Virgilian influence extended beyond verbal borrowing to the techniques of scenic design discussed in the previous chapter.

The Carolingian material considered below is restricted to three poems, the anonymous *Karolus Magnus et Leo Papa*, Ermoldus Nigellus' *In Honorem Hludowici*, and the *Waltharius*, which may or may not be the work of a certain unidentified Geraldus. The first of these poems is topical and provides indices which date it in the summer of 799.[1] Ermoldus' poem is also topical and must have

---

[1] See *Karolus Magnus et Leo Papa: Ein Paderborner Epos vom Jahre 799*, mit Beiträgen von Helmut Beumann, Franz Brunhölzl, Wilhelm Winkelmann, Studien und Quellen zur westfälischen Geschichte 8 (Paderborn, 1966), pp. 7–12.

been written between 826 and 828.[2] The *Waltharius,* on
the other hand, is a Latin elaboration of an undatable
Germanic heroic legend and provides no sound chrono-
logical indications. Arguments have been offered for the
first half of the tenth century, the second half of the ninth
century, and, more recently, the first half of the ninth
century.[3] Although specific arguments seem to cancel each
other out, the last verdict is attractive on the general
grounds that the poem is most readily comprehensible in
the context of early ninth-century literary activity and becomes decreasingly plausible as time goes on. A century
later it would be an isolated phenomenon, and in the
waning ninth century it does not sort well with such narrative efforts as Abbo's mannered *Siege of Paris* or the Poeta
Saxo's verse annals *Gesta Caroli Magni.* On the other
hand, it does accord well with the first bloom of Charlemagne's revival as well as with his interest in Germanic
traditions at the beginning of the century. I will therefore
treat the three poems as approximately contemporaneous,
while the reader should be forewarned that there may be
a gap of more than a hundred years should the *Waltharius*
turn out to be a tenth-century composition after all.

Karolus Magnus et Leo Papa

Karolus Magnus et Leo Papa is a poem of 536 hexa-
meters describing Charlemagne's reception of Pope Leo at

---

[2] See *Ermold le noir: Poème sur Louis le pieux et épîtres au roi Pépin,*
ed. Edmond Faral, Les Classiques de l'histoire de France au moyen âge
(Paris, 1932), p. viii.

[3] A convenient collection of essays bearing on the problem is *Waltharius
und Walthersage: Eine Dokumentation der Forschung,* ed. Emil Ernst
Ploss (Hildesheim: Georg Olms, 1969). The most recent of several *For-
schungsberichte* is Karl Langosch, *Waltharius: Die Dichtung und die Forschung,* Erträge der Forschung 21 (Darmstadt: Wissenschaftliche Buchgesellschaft, 1973).

Paderborn shortly after political turbulence in Rome had
cast doubt on the pontiff's survival in office. Decorative
passages in praise of Charlemagne and his works precede
the section of the poem narrating a conference between
the pope and the Frankish king. Chief among these works
is the palace at Aachen, where the king is presented as he
surveys the progress of the construction (vv. 97–98):

> Stat pius arce procul Karolus loca singula signans,
> Altaque disponens venturae moenia Romae.
>
> (Clement Charles stands on the citadel pointing out in-
> dividual sites and making dispositions for the lofty walls
> of a Rome about to rise.)

The king's perspective is a combination of Aeneas' view of
the construction at Carthage in 1. 421–29 and his super-
vision of the work in 4. 260. The station atop a citadel is
reminiscent of Laocoon's lookout in 2. 41 (*summa decurrit
ab arce*) and Dido's view of Aeneas' preparations for departure in 4. 410 (*arce ex summa*). One may question
whether it is practicable to combine the proximity required of a supervisor guiding his workmen with the
eagle's perspective of an onlooker posted on a citadel, but
the point is that our poet has learned the Virgilian trick
of deploying a panoramic scene. He creates the illusion
that the following passage is seen from and dominated by
the superior vantage point established for Charlemagne.

The description of the construction site is close Virgilian imitation: the location of the senate (v. 99 = 1. 426),
the raising of a citadel and the transport of building
materials by hand (vv. 102–3 = 1. 424), the digging of a
harbor and the construction of theater foundations (vv.
104–5 =1. 427–28), and the building of a great church
(v. 112 = 1. 446) all have correspondences in the *Aeneid*.

The scene concludes with an adaptation of Virgil's bee simile to summarize the industry of the workers (vv. 127–36). Some of the specific building projects are dubious in Charlemagne's Aachen, but by literary standards the scene is lively. Its vitality stems not so much from an imitation of Virgil's details as from an imitation of his play with lines and perspectives, the intersecting of vertical and horizontal planes, the upward thrust of citadel and columns, and the downward plunge of excavations. The construction of a temple provides mass (*ingenti . . . molimine*), but the mass loses its weight when it is projected heavenward (*scandit ad astra*). This interplay is derivative and unconscious, but in the area of animation the poet deliberately exceeds his model. Virgil is content with relatively sedate *parts . . . pars* and *hic alii . . . hic alii* coordinates to suggest the swirl of activity.[4] His Carolingian imitator multiplies the commotion. There are eight such coordinates (vv. 101, 103, 106, 111, 114, 117, 118, 125), and these are reinforced by new effects. One innovation is the note of nervous emulousness introduced into the labor by the use of the words *certo* and *certatim:*

> Ast alii rupes manibus subvolvere certant [v. 103]
> Construere ingenti templum molimine certant [v. 112]
> Materiam Romae certatim congregat altae [v. 124]

The device itself is Virgilian (for example, *Aen.* 2. 64, 2. 628, 3. 290, 7. 146, 7. 472, 7. 585, 10. 130), but the concentration in one passage is new and produces a surplus of scenic energy as one man strives to outdo the next.

Twice the poet describes the work force as *operosa cohors* (vv. 101, 123), and in the latter instance he conveys

[4] On this device see Richard Heinze, *Virgils epische Technik*, 3d ed. (Leipzig and Berlin: Teubner, 1915; rpt. Darmstadt: Wissenschaftliche Buchgesellschaft, 1957), p. 356.

both the orderly rhythm and the random deployment of
the laborers:

> Itque reditque operosa cohors, diffusa per urbem.

> (The company of workers comes and goes, spread through
> the city.)

At the same time, the poet creates a new perpendicularity
by describing workers high atop the church, seconded by
other workers in a descending line (vv. 114–18):

> Pars super in summis populi procul arcibus ardens
> Saxa locat, solido coniungens marmora nexu;
> Altera stat gradibus portantum sorte receptans
> Pars onera, atque avidis manibus praedura ministrat
> Saxa; alii subeunt, volvunt ad moenia rupes;

> (One group diligently places the stones above in the
> highest towers, firmly joining the marble blocks, another
> group stands on the scaffolding receiving in turn the
> burden of the bearers and managing the unyielding
> stones with eager hands; others approach from below
> and convey the blocks to the walls.)

Noise, as well as motion, is a familiar phenomenon on a
construction site and must have been so even before the
days of high-decibel machinery. Virgil suggests it with the
single word *strepitus* (1. 422), but his Carolingian heir
again multiplies the effect (vv. 121–22):

> Plaustraque dant sonitum; vastus fragor aethera pulsat;
> Fit strepitus, magna consurgit stridor in urbe:

> (The wagons clatter, a vast din strikes the heavens, there
> is an uproar, and a clamor gathers and rises in the great
> city.)

The comparison with Virgil reveals that the Carolingian poet has introduced more noise, energy, and diversity into the scene, partly by simple repetition and partly by varying the techniques of his model. We may leave it to the arbiters of taste to judge whether the gain in energy is worth the loss in harmony, but two failures in the elaboration should be noted. In the first place, the uncertainty as to whether Charlemagne is actually on the site guiding the work or high above the site observing it deprives us of the visionlike quality of Aeneas' view from an overlooking hill. This distance makes the reduced scale of Virgil's bee simile appropriate. In the Carolingian counterpart the distance is less certain and the appropriateness of the bee simile a little less evident. At the same time, although the scene is technically viewed from Charlemagne's stance, this perspective is less strictly adhered to than in the *Aeneid*. In the latter case the passage begins with the words *miratur molem Aeneas* (1. 421), immediately echoed in the following line (*miratur portas strepitumque*). and ends with Aeneas' exclamation (1. 437):

o fortunati, quorum iam moenia surgunt!

(Oh happy are they for whom walls already rise!)

We are thus reminded that we are observing the scene through Aeneas' eyes, while in the later poem Charlemagne is allowed to slip out of focus, and the scene becomes independent of the onlooker. Virgilian technique dictates in general that a landscape or a scene should open up before the eye of an onlooker and that the image should be focused through his eye as it registers fear, relief, admiration, or some other state of mind inspired by the view. In the present instance, the protracted hardship of

Aeneas' mission flashes through his mind as he looks down at the fulfilled scene below and ponders the fulfillment which for him lies at best in the dim future. Both the carefully executed visual revelation and the accompanying mental revelation, which are characteristically combined in Virgil's scenic procedures, are absent from the Carolingian poem. To be sure, it shares in the Carolingian *renovatio* ideal (Modoin of Autun's *aurea Roma iterum renovata renascitur orbi*) as Charlemagne lays out the *venturae moenia Romae* (v. 98), but the vision is communicated by the poet; it is not conveyed as a part of the king's experience as he gazes over the site.

Karolus Magnus et Leo Papa pursues the scene in close imitation of Virgil's Carthage (vv. 137–39 = *Aen.* 1. 441):

> Non procul excelsa nemus est et amoena virecta
> Lucus ab urbe virens et prata recentia rivis
> Obtinet in medio, multis circumsita muris.

> (Not far from the peerless city there is a wood and a pleasant lawn, in their midst a green grove and meadows near the banks, surrounded by many walls.)

Whereas the grove in Carthage is a temple site within the city, the grove at Aachen is a preserve outside the city given over to exercise and hunting (vv. 150–52). It is therefore larger and less surveyable than Virgil's grove, but the poet has made allowance for the expansion. In the *Aeneid* the perspective is altered and the grove becomes a close-up as Aeneas proceeds through the city in his protective cloud. In the imitation the distance is not canceled, and there is a lingering impression that the park is seen from Charlemagne's citadel.

Like the previous passage, this one undergoes an exu-

berant elaboration of the scene, pieced together from other
Virgilian passages and aimed at enlivening an otherwise
static landscape. Motion is added by referring to the grove
revealed before Aeneas as his ship approaches the mouth
of the Tiber at the beginning of Book 7. This sight is
animated by the wheeling and singing of birds (7. 29–34):

> atque hic Aeneas ingentem ex aequore lucum
> prospicit. hunc inter fluuio Tiberinus amoeno
> uerticibus rapidis et multa flauus harena
> in mare prorumpit. uariae circumque supraque
> adsuetae ripis uolucres et fluminis alueo
> aethera mulcebant cantu lucoque uolabant.

(And here Aeneas perceives a great grove arising from
the sea. From it the Tiber tawny with sand flows into
the sea with a pleasant stream and rapid eddies. Above
and about a variety of birds, which haunt the banks and
the basin and the grove, were wheeling and sweetening
the air with their song.)

So, too, the Carolingian poet animates his grove (vv. 140–
43):

> Hic amnem circumvolitat genus omne volucrum;
> In ripis resident rimantes pascua rostris;
> Nunc procul in medio summergunt flumine sese,
> Nunc quoque praecipiti properant ad litora cursu;

(Here all varieties of birds wheel about the stream; they
stand on the banks grubbing for food with their bills;
now they dive far off in the midst of the river, now they
set a headlong course for the shores.)

At this point it may be useful to cast a glance back at the
total tradition. Neither the river mouth as a landing site

nor the birds as an animating device is Virgil's invention.
The river mouth is inherited from Odysseus' arrival on
Scheria (5. 441–44):

> But when he came swimming to the mouth of a
> Fair-flowing river, it seemed the best place,
> Free of rocks and sheltered from the wind;
> He recognized it flowing out and prayed in his spirit.

The reader will recall that the whole sequence concerned
with Odysseus' landing is internalized and viewed in terms
of the hero's sensations. Landscape features are mentioned
only inasmuch as they dictate Odysseus' state of mind.
Thus the fair-flowing river has no decorative dimensions;
the only features that occur to the poet are smoothness and
windlessness because these features promise safety to the
much-buffeted swimmer. Virgil, on the other hand, with
his pictorial eye, takes his key from the stock adjective
"fair-flowing," renders it with *fluuio amoeno*, adds grove
and birds, and creates a little idyll to welcome Aeneas to
his destination.

The birds, too, are traditional. We may trace them to
Homer's simile in the *Iliad* II. 459–65, in which they convey the massing of the Greek soldiery:

> Like the great flocks of winged birds,
> Of geese and of cranes and of long-necked swans,
> In the Asian meadow and along the waters of the Caÿster,
> Wheeling hither and thither, delighting in flight
> And alighting with cries, and the meadow resounds,
> So did the great companies from the ships and the tents
> Pour out on the Scamandrian plain.

From this passage Virgil takes the pictures of birds
sweeping over banks and waters. But already in the *Odyssey* the birds had been demoblized and assigned to a new

context in the *locus amoenus* around Calypso's cave (5. 65–67):

> There long-winged birds nested,
> Horned owls and hawks and long-tongued cormorants,
> Which are busy with the works of the sea.

Virgil combines both passages, the movement of the Iliadic simile with the tranquillity of the Odyssean pleasance, to create Aeneas' gently animated vision of the Tiber. But one important change was necessary to effect the transformation. Homer's selection of geese, cranes, swans, and owls suggests a cacophonous hooting and honking for which Virgil had no use (as he did later in 7. 699–705). He therefore leaves the birds unspecified and is free to imagine a melodious twittering.

The Carolingian poet adheres to Virgil's flight indications (*circumque supraque . . . uolabant = amnem circumvolitat*) and his generic generality (*uariae . . . uolucres = genus omne volucrum*), but in his quest for additional scenic energy he combines these features with yet another Virgilian passage (*Georgics* 1. 383–89), which also echoes the simile in Book II of the *Iliad:*

> iam uariae pelagi uolucres et quae Asia circum
> dulcibus in stagnis rimantur prata Caystri—
> certatim largos umeris infundere rores,
> nunc caput obiectare fretis, nunc currere in undas
> et studio incassum uideas gestire lauandi.
> tum cornix plena pluuiam uocat improba uoce
> et sola in sicca secum spatiatur harena.

> (Then there are the various birds of the sea, which grub in the sweet pools about the Asian meadows of the Caÿster; they emulously cover their backs with showers of spray, now they dive headlong in the waters, now

they run into the waves and you may see them wantonly
sporting in their eagerness to bathe. Then the villain-
ous crow calls down the rain with full voice and stalks
alone on the dry sand.)

These verses provide the Carolingian imitator with the
search for food and the busy traffic on the water and along
the banks, the kind of activity and familiar detail that completely alter the decorative stillness of the river scene at the
outset of the Seventh *Aeneid*. As in the lines devoted to
Charlemagne's construction, the object is to create a fuller
and livelier canvas.

To the same end, animal life is added to the bird life
already described (vv. 144–48):

Hosque toros iuxta cervorum pascitur agmen
Riparum in longa per amoenaque pascua valle.
Huc illuc timido discurrit dammula gressu:
Fronde retecta vacat; passim genus omne ferarum
His latet in silvis.

(By the hillocks of the banks an antlered herd grazes
along the pleasant pastures in the long valley. Hither
and thither a little deer runs with timid steps, leaving
the cover of the wood; everywhere in these forests there
lurk all manner of beasts.)

The deer are borrowed from yet another passage in the
Aeneid (1. 184–86) and ultimately from the *Odyssey* (10.
156–59), providing a fuller comparative perspective, which
we need not pursue. It is sufficient to note that the Carolingian poet once again opts for animation: he alters the
stateliness of Virgil's quietly browsing herd by introducing
the timid darting hither and thither of a little deer.

The park thus stocked with wildlife serves as a background for a hunting sequence modeled closely on the fateful hunt in the *Aeneid* 4. The establishment of a scenic

background is characteristic of Virgil's methods, and the Carolingian poet follows this lead to the fullest extent. By coalescing passages from *Aeneid* 1 and 4, he creates a total landscape that encompasses everything in sight, first the confines of the city, then the park beyond, and finally, as the stage is set for the hunt, the mountains still further in the distance (vv. 153–56):

> Exoritur radiis cum primum Phoebus honestis,
> Et iubar ignicomo perlustrat lumine montes,
> Praecipites scopulos et summa cacumina tangens
> Silvarum . . .

> (When Phoebus first rises with splendid rays and the orb illumines the mountains with the light of fiery locks, touching the precipitous summits and the topmost peaks of the forests . . .)

The sunrise corresponds to the *Aeneid* 4. 129–30, but the scenery is from other Virgilian passages. The *scopuli* and *silvae* are from 1. 163–66 and the *summa cacumina* from 6. 678. The effect is to create a mountain backdrop for the scene, as Virgil does when describing Aeneas' landing in Libya, a background against which the hunt may be played out in an area defined by the city on one side and the mountains beyond. Against this background the poet assembles his huntsmen, with a close reliance on *Aeneid* 4. 130–50, but with a more than fivefold expansion (vv. 156–269). The expansion is achieved largely by the introduction of a series of notables, first Charlemagne, then his queen Liutgard, his sons Charles and Pippin, and his daughters Rotrud, Bertha, Gisela, Rothaid, Theodrada, and Hiltrud. The original hunting scene is broadened considerably. Virgil was intent on setting Dido and Aeneas in relief against the mass of hunters, but his Carolingian successor was faced with a variety of panegyric obligations and

responded with a canvas which suffers from the repetitiveness of a parade scene. Nonetheless, the technique remains
Virgilian, as a few examples will show. The impatience
and anticipation rendered in the *Aeneid* 4. 135 by the
bridled eagerness of Dido's steed, while her nobles await
her appearance, recur (vv. 157–58):

> . . . resistit
> Nobilium manus expectans in limine primo.

> (The band of nobles stands expectantly on the edge of
> the threshold.)

The eagerness of the hunting horse becomes more explicit
in the imitation (v. 167):

> Stans movet acre caput, montes cupit ire per altos.

> (Standing there he tosses his head impatiently and longs
> to course through the high mountains.)

Virgil is content to mention the presence of hunting dogs
(4. 132: *odora canum uis*), but the Carolingian elaboration
allows them to share the horse's impatience as they are held
in check (vv. 175–76):

> Atque canes avidos ducunt per colla revinctos,
> Ad praedam faciles furiosoque ore molosos.

> (And they lead the eager dogs leashed by their collars,
> mastiffs bent on their quarry and baying furiously.)

There is a repressed energy in the scene, more insistent
than Virgil's controlled picture, and the energy is released
more emphatically. Virgil's account of the ride out is
neutral to the point of being grammatically impersonal
(4. 151; contrast 12. 121–23), but in the Carolingian scene

the hunting party practically bursts from the gates (vv. 179–81): [5]

> . . . alte urbis panduntur classica portae
> Cornua concrepitant, fragor ingens atria complet,
> Praecipitique ruunt iuvenes ad litora cursu.

(The gates of the city are thrown open [the line as a whole is ungrammatical]; the horns blare, a great din fills the court, and the youths rush headlong to the shores.)

The passage goes on to emphasize the noise which, as on the construction site, dominates the scene (vv. 159–64, 208–11):

> Fit strepitus, clamor consurgit vastus in urbe;
> Desuper ex alto respondent culmine tecta
> Aerea; praecipuus conscendit stridor in auras;
> Hinnit equusque ad equum, conclamat turba pedestris,
> Inque vicem proprio revocatur pignore quisque
> Ad dominum famulusque suum sequiturque vocantem.

(There is an uproar, a great din mounts in the city; above the brazen roofs echo from their peaks; a sharp clamor rises into the air; one horse whinnies to another, the crowd on foot shouts confusedly, each calls the other by name, and servants follow masters calling after them.)

> . . . certatim exire senatus
> Conatur magno cum murmuris inde tumultu.
> Cornua rauca sonant, avido latratibus auras
> Conplent ore canes, fragor ignea sidera pulsat.

(The courtiers press forth in a great throng with a hum of voices. The harsh trumpets resound, the dogs with

[5] The same sort of animation is characteristic of a later German rendering by Friedrich Schiller. See his *Sämtliche Werke* (Munich: Carl Hanser, 1959), III, 431.

eager throats fill the air with their baying, a din strikes
the starry heavens.)

The clamor, the baying trumpets, the reverberating heavens, in short, all the exalted touches, are Virgil's. But the
more intimate details, the horses whinnying to each other,
the rowdy pedestrians, people calling one another by name,
servants scampering after shouting masters, and dogs com-
pleting the pandemonium with their barks, these are the
Carolingian additions. They convey a sense of common
reality which the poet manages to combine with Virgil's
lofty outlines without creating incongruities and with a
pleasant gain in liveliness and immediacy.

The common touch is suppressed in dealing with the
royal personages who participate in the hunt. We may take
Charlemagne himself as an example (vv. 168–72):

> Egreditur tandem; circum stipante caterva,
> Europae veneranda pharus es prodit ad auram.
> Enitet eximio vultu facieque coruscat;
> Nobile namque caput pretioso amplectitur auro
> Rex Karolus; cunctos humeris supereminet altis.

> (He emerges at last; surrounded by a thronging crowd,
> the venerated beacon of Europe makes his appearance.
> His countenance is resplendent and his visage brilliant,
> for the noble head of King Charles is encircled with
> precious gold; he rises head and shoulders above all his
> companions.)

These lines contain no fewer than four Virgilian techniques for setting off the appearance of an individual, the
first and fourth from Virgil's description of Dido and the
second and third from his description of Aeneas. The first
is what I have termed centripetal design, the focusing of a
stately center by suggesting a moving periphery. Virgil

uses the device in describing Dido, both when she first appears to Aeneas (1. 497) and in the hunting scene (4. 136). The second is the glowing countenance which Virgil attributes to Aeneas (4. 150), while the golden head adornment is borrowed from the figure of Apollo in the simile used to supplement Aeneas' portrayal (4. 147–48). Finally, the last line borrows the device of supereminence from the figure of Diana leading the dance in the simile that describes Dido's first appearance (1. 500). The poet has drawn on two Books and two figures (or four, if Apollo and Diana should be tallied separately), on direct descriptions as well as on similes, in order to provide the maximum stature for Charlemagne. The result, though more concentrated and more massive, is decidedly less fine than Virgil's portraiture, but it is in proportion to the increased confusion and tumult of the Carolingian canvas, which requires a more determined effort to disengage the principal figures before the reader's eye.

These techniques for setting individuals in relief fairly exhaust the Virgilian resources, and they are simply repeated in order to focus other prominent participants in the hunt. Liutgard is the center of a crowd, rosy-complexioned, and richly adorned (vv. 182–94). Pippin is centered, bright-faced, and gold-crowned (vv. 200–206). Rotrud is crowned and richly attired (vv. 213–18). Bertha is centered, adorned with a golden diadem, and otherwise brilliantly decked out (vv. 220–28). Gisela has all these assets in addition to a brilliant complexion and eyes which surpass the brightness of the sun (vv. 229–42). Rothaid is encrusted with gems (vv. 243–50), while Theodrada's splendor owes more to the natural coloring of forehead, hair, feet, hands, mouth, cheeks, neck, and eyes (vv. 251–62).

The fullblown description of personal appearance in

Karolus Magnus et Leo Papa extends to the natural scenery as well. Virgil gives a brief and reasonably lucid account of the chase (4. 151–59): when the hunters have arrived in the mountainous wilds, they start the goats from a ridge above, while herds of deer leave the mountains and traverse the open fields. In the meantime, Ascanius exults on his horse in the valley, spurning the hooved beasts and hoping for a boar or a lion. The picture is clear. Animals have been driven from the higher elevations to the huntsmen in the open valleys below.

What happens to this clear scheme in the Carolingian elaboration is a masterpiece of unsurveyability (vv. 270–90). The mountain wilds and level valleys are spun out into high-lying woods *(lustra alta)*, dense shrubbery *(condensa frutecta)*, dark glades *(opaci saltus)*, forests *(silvae)*, the glade again *(saltus)*, a valley *(vallis)*, a grove *(nemus)*, the dark silences of the forest *(opaca silentia silvae)*, more shady shrubbery *(umbrosa frutecta)*, more glades, more forests, and vast areas *(loca vasta)*, trackless stretches *(invia)*, and high mountain peaks *(alta cacumina montis)*. The action begins with five lines of scenting and searching by the eager hounds. Then the huntsmen deploy themselves and discover a boar in a valley. They plunge after it in hot pursuit, and the hounds join the chase. Five more lines describe the postures and various degrees of efficiency in the dogs, while the boar, tearing the foliage as it goes, heads for the mountain peaks. As it is brought to bay and turns on the dogs, Charlemagne advances, fleeter than the birds, and dispatches the beast with his sword while his children watch from a mountain.

In general, the hunt is located in mountainous and heavily wooded terrain, but the boar is started in a valley and makes for the heights, where it is brought to bay while others observe, whether from another mountain or from a higher point on the same mountain is not clear. Aside from much additional vegetation, which is more chaotic than scenic, the most significant departure from Virgil is a strong interest in the details and mechanics of the hunt, notably the behavior of the hounds (cf. *Georgics* 3. 404–13) and the rampaging pursuit. This is once more in line with the tendency toward specific realism in *Karolus Magnus et Leo Papa*. Virgil, on the other hand, was not interested in the blood sport as such and chose to sum up the mood of the chase by emphasizing Ascanius' high spirits, a characteristic internalizing of the action.

Charlemagne concludes the hunt with an open-air banquet arranged for his companions in tents pitched in a shady grove (vv. 314–25). This has at most an analogy in Evander's sylvan feast (8. 175–83), but the situation is likely to have been authentic in view of what we learn from Einhard about Charlemagne's predilection for hunting, the outdoor life, and simple fare.[6]

The changes that the Carolingian poet operated on his Virgilian model may be summarized in terms of vigor, abundance, and an infusion of ordinariness. But these are minor revisions in the context of a strong scenic continuity. Symptomatic of the close adherence to the Virgilian scenic instinct is the moment at which the hunt concludes under the eyes of Charlemagne's children. Although the location of the mountain lookout is uncertain, the poet clearly is responding to the Virgilian habit of visualizing panoramic scenes through the eye of a beholder posted on

---

[6] On the cultivated simplicity of Evander's banquet see Heinze, *Virgils epische Technik*, pp. 488–89. On Charlemagne's habits: *Einhardi Vita Karoli Magni*, post G. H. Pertz recensuit G. Waitz, curavit O. Holder-Egger, Scriptores rerum germanicarum (Hanover: Impensis Bibliopolii Hahniani, 1911 [Neudruck 1927]), chaps. 22, 24 (pp. 27–29).

a commanding vantage point. This type of scenic consciousness is inherited from Virgil and maintained remarkably well intact.

Ermoldus Nigellus' *In Honorem Hludowici*

Ermoldus' poem maintains the scenic heritage much less well. Indeed, it is the pale copy of a copy since its scenery is less dependent on Virgil than on the reflections of Virgil in *Karolus Magnus et Leo Papa*. It represents a filtering and diluting of the tradition quite opposite to the efforts at enrichment in the earlier Carolingian poem.

Ermoldus describes in the four books of his poem a series of major events prior to and during the first half of Louis the Pious' reign, the siege of Barcelona in 800, Louis' accession to the throne in 814 and consecration in 816, his campaign against the Bretons in 818, and his reception and conversion of the Danish King Harald at Ingelheim in 826. Most of the narrative is reported, not staged, and provides little scope for scenery, at least in the first three books. A few localizations are introduced in a stereotyped manner:

> Est locus insignis . . . [v. 230]
> Trans fluvium Ligeris locus est . . . [v. 744]
> Dicitur Inda locus . . . [v. 1238]
> Est locus . . . [v. 1346]
> Est urbs . . . [v. 1504]
> Est locus insignis . . . [v. 1836]

This particular convention, inherited from Virgil (for example *Aen.* 1. 159, 2. 21, 3. 163, 5. 124, 8. 597, 11. 316, 11. 522) and ultimately from Homer (for example, *Il.* vi. 152, *Od.* 3. 293, 4. 354, 4. 844, 13. 96, 19. 172), opens a

long perspective on metamorphoses in scenic design.[7] The
Homeric instances are associated with brief and incon-
spicuous passages and are exhausted within a few lines.
The first one referred to above belongs in the familiar
speech of Glaucus as he confronts Diomedes; the introduction of the city of Ephyra serves merely to preface his
genealogy. The second example sets the scene for the destruction of some of Menelaus' ships on the way to Egypt,
a minor event reported to Telemachus by Nestor. The
third example belongs to Menelaus' own report of his
detention in Egypt. The fourth indicates the location of
the rocky island by which the suitors lie in wait for Telemachus—an ambush that comes to nothing and is part of
the awkward seam between Telemachy and Odysseus' adventures. The last example is part of the Cretan fiction
which Odysseus, as yet unidentified, spins in reply to
Penelope's inquiry about his origins. All of these settings
are incidental.

In Virgil's usage scenic ecphrasis acquires altogether new
dimensions. The first example above sets the scene for the
brilliantly landscaped approach to Libya, the second for
the sinister night attack on Troy, the fourth for the elaborately described boat race, and the last for the ambush of
Aeneas, which, perhaps in mock imitation of *Od.* 4. 844,
never materializes. This last example is most significant for
Ermoldus, departing from the islands and skerries of the
Odyssey and the Odyssean *Aeneid* to create an inland setting (11. 522–29):

[7] On the use of the formula see R. G. Austin, ed., *P. Vergili Maronis
Aeneidos Liber Quartus* (Oxford: Clarendon, 1955), p. 143; Gordon Williams, *Tradition and Originality in Roman Poetry* (Oxford: Clarendon,
1968), pp. 651–54; Charles Paul Segal, *Landscape in Ovid's Metamorphoses:
A Study in the Transformations of a Literary Symbol,* Hermes Einzel-
schriften 23 (Wiesbaden: Franz Steiner, 1969), p. 7.

Est curuo anfractu ualles, accommoda fraudi
armorumque dolis, quam densis frondibus atrum
urget utrimque latus, tenuis quo semita ducit
angustaeque ferunt fauces aditusque maligni.
hanc super in speculis summoque in uertice montis
planities ignota iacet tutique receptus,
seu dextra laeuaque uelis occurrere pugnae
siue instare iugis et grandia uoluere saxa.

(There is a winding valley, well adapted for ambush and
the stratagems of armed men, confined on both sides by
slopes dark with dense cover, and into which leads a
narrow path and tight walls and a menacing access.
Above it on the heights and the very summit of the rise
there lies an invisible plateau and a safe gathering place
from which to initiate battle either from the left or the
right or to stand on the ridges and roll down great
boulders.)

Such a descriptive digression evoking a detailed and variously accidented landscape is quite unlike anything in
Homer: a winding valley, thickly overgrown slopes, a narrow path on the floor of the valley, a tight entrance to the
pass, and an overhanging summit surmounted by a flat
ridge which recedes out of sight. The complex of straight
and twisting, abrupt and protracted, rising and retreating
lines combine to give a remarkably full picture of a mountainous setting.

In a passage describing the situation of the monastery at
Conques, Ermoldus outlines a valley accessible over a
rocky path, but the poverty of scenic resources is in striking contrast (vv. 238–41):

Valle sedet magna, praecincta flumine amoeno,
    Vinetis, pomis, seu dapibus variis.
Rupibus excisis valido sudante labore,
    Quo pateat locus hic, semita rege datur.

(It is located in a large valley, bordered by a pleasant
river, by vineyards, fruits, and various crops. A road is
constructed by the king, carved out of the rock at the
cost of great labor, to provide access to the place.)

There are no echoes of Virgil in the passage and certainly
no trace of the interplay of landscape lines, only a river
and a little vegetation, but Ermoldus expands in another
direction. He tells us that prior to the building of the
monastery, the valley was a haunt for beasts and melodious
birds (v. 232: *Olim namque feris avibusque canoribus
aptus*), and in so doing he follows the lead of *Karolus
Magnus et Leo Papa* by enlivening the scene with a detail
taken from the *Georgics* (2. 328: *auia tum resonant auibus
uirgulta canoris*). He reverts several times to this type of
animation in describing the location of Louis' palace at
Doué (v. 747: *Piscibus est habilis, est loculesque feris*),
or the foundation at Inde (vv. 1242–43: *Cornigeris quon-
dam sedes gratissima cervis, Ursis seu bubalis apta, ferisque
capris*), or the city of Vannes (v. 1507: *Pisce repleta . . .*),
or the hunting park at Aachen inherited directly from
Karolus Magnus et Leo Papa (vv. 1840–47: *Hunc volucres
variae incolitantque ferae*, etc.).

These landscapes are distinguished from Virgil's, or
even from those of *Karolus Magnus et Leo Papa,* by the
poet's failure to exploit them. We are told simply that
there is a place at Conques where Louis built a monastery,
or that there is a place at Doué where Louis built a palace.
No action ensues. The last instance, involving the hunting
park at Aachen, is particularly instructive. The poet of
Karolus Magnus described a hunting area because he was
about to describe a hunt; it was appropriate that the setting should be filled with birds and beasts. This is not so
in the case of Ermoldus. His description of wildlife is quite
beside the point because in his poem the park is to be the

scene not of a hunt, but of a judicial duel—a not untypical example of the mechanical procedures in Ermoldus' imitations. Only once does he integrate his action into a setting established for the purpose.

The passage in question occurs in the last book and involves Louis' ceremonial reception of King Harald at his palace in Ingelheim. The introductory formula is the usual one (v. 2062):

> Est locus ille situs rapidi prope flumina Rheni.

> (The place is located by the stream of the swift-flowing Rhine.)

There follows a brief and formalized description of the palace and church which are to be the chief scenes of the state visit. Here the reader, accustomed to earlier truncated descriptions, is surprised to find that the passage goes on for nearly 100 lines (vv. 2070–2163) to detail the pictures of sacred and secular events with which the church is adorned. This view is inspired by the frieze in Dido's temple depicting Trojan events (1. 456–93), but again the imitation is mechanical. Aeneas' pictorial vision of the Trojan calamity serves to revive his harsh memories and his sense of temporary release from past hardships, while suggesting that his name and fate are already known in Carthage, thus providing a sympathetic bond between the Carthaginian queen and himself. Ermoldus' frieze is purely ornamental, calculated at most to promote dumb wonder at Louis' opulence and the kind of awe in King Harald which will make him more amenable to conversion.

Having concluded the description, Ermoldus, once more departing from earlier practice, does not allow the scenery to lapse, but introduces Harald into it (vv. 2168–70):

> Ecce volant centum per Rheni flumina puppes,
>   Velaque candidolis consociata modis,[8]
> Denorum populis oneratae, munere nec non;

(Lo there fly through the waters of the Rhine a hundred ships, a crowd of sails glistening white [?], loaded with the Danish race, and bearing gifts.)

The opening words are borrowed, oddly enough, from Virgil's foot race (5. 324), and they make vivid use of the interjection and present tense: the Danish fleet bursts onto the scene, giving our sense of the surroundings no time to fade and focusing our attention on the ships through the suddenness with which they appear and the speed of their advance. Their materialization on the horizon is observed by Louis in his palace (vv. 2174–75):

> Jamque propinquabant ripae portumque tenebant;
>   Caesar ab excelsa haec prospicit arce pius . . .

(Already they were approaching the bank and heading for port; the clement Emperor views this from his commanding citadel . . .)

This scene is yet another draft on Virgil. The sighting of ships as they advance down a river is a notion borrowed from the *Aeneid* 8. 107–8, a passage in which Virgil uses complementary perspectives as he first visualizes Aeneas approaching Evander's realm and catching sight of walls and citadel, then focuses on Evander and Pallas outside the city walls as they conduct a sacrifice to Hercules and in turn catch sight of the approaching ships. Ermoldus avails

8 I prefer Dümmler's reading *modis* in *Poetae Latini Aevi Carolini*, II (Berolini: Apud Weidmannos, 1884), 66 (v. 288) to Faral's *nodis* (the edition cited in footnote 2, p. 166). Neither makes much sense, but *modis* is at least metrical.

himself only of the perspective from city to ships, but he converts Evander's citadel, the landmark sighted by Aeneas, to his own uses by transforming it into Louis' lookout point. The thought lay near at hand since a citadel serves as lookout post both in the *Aeneid* 4. 410 and in *Karolus Magnus et Leo Papa* v. 97.

The following sequence shows a continued and far-reaching dependence on the scenery and phraseology of the Evander episode. Louis' dispatching of Matfrid to accompany Harald from the ships (vv. 2176–81) is a reflection of Pallas' role in 8. 122–25. When Harald first addresses Louis (v. 2186), he is following Aeneas' example (8. 127), and when he offers to identify *Meque domumque meam, et genus omne simul* (v. 2187), he is responding not to the requirements of the situation, since Louis has undertaken the diplomatic initiative and knows Harald's background very well, but to Pallas' interrogation of Aeneas (8. 114: *qui genus? unde domo?*) and ultimately to the corresponding Homeric formula (for example, *Od.* 1. 170, 10. 325). When Louis immediately and apparently without motivation offers refreshments (v. 2183: *Ordinat expensas distribuitque dapes*), he is following the example of Evander, who logically invites his Trojan guests to participate in the sacrificial feast which has already been prepared (8. 175–76: . . . *dapes iubet et sublata reponi pocula* . . .). Finally, when Harald launches into a description of his heathen rites (vv. 2190–97), he is not inspired by a question of Louis' but by Evander's explanation of the sacrifice to Hercules in which the Arcadians are engaged (8. 185–275).

Following the introductory niceties, the first order of the day is to baptize Harald and his retinue. Then Franks and Danes make their way to a church service in a procession modeled on *Karolus Magnus et Leo Papa*. The only Vir-

gilian descriptive technique which survives this transmission is the one which interested the Roman poet least—the
itemizing of splendid attire.[9] The church, so clearly intended to amaze Harald, has the desired effect (vv. 2318–
23):

> Miratur Herold, conjunx mirantur et omnes,
>   Proles et socii, culmina tanta Dei;
> Mirantur clerum, mirantur denique templum . . .

> (Harald marvels, his wife and all his children and com-
> panions marvel at such a great house of God; they mar-
> vel at the clergy, they marvel at the church itself . . .)

The anaphora is inherited from Aeneas' admiration of
Carthage (1. 421–22), but once again the Virgilian fullness
is drained. Aeneas' wonder is that of an exiled man suddenly returned to civilization and a homeless man suddenly confronted with a thriving colony. Harald's wonder
has no such psychological value and is a mere foil to Ermoldus' obsequious praise of Louis' opulence and Chris-
tian pomp. It is entirely in the spirit of the piece that the
poet breaks into a direct apostrophe of Harald, asking him
which religion he *now* prefers after seeing such a glittering
display. And it is equally in the spirit of the poem that the
day concludes with a banquet that emphasizes the magnifi-
cence of food, wine, and tableware, in contrast to Dido's
banquet, the model for the passage, which emphasizes not
exterior splendor, but a special mingling of emotions.

In conjunction with the banquet Ermoldus can make
no use either of Aeneas' apologue or of the haunted night
that Dido spends after hearing the story. He is therefore

---

[9] Brooks Otis argues a negative tonality in the passage which ultimately
serves as a model for the finery and jewels of vv. 2254–79 (*Virgil: A Study
in Civilized Poetry* [Oxford: Clarendon, 1963], p. 80): "We see her [Dido's]
horse and attire, but not her heart."

somewhat at a loss in making the transition to the following day, on which, true to the pattern established in the
Aeneid and *Karolus Magnus et Leo Papa,* a hunt is sched-
uled. As a result, he terminates the banquet abruptly (vv.
2360–61), stating only that it was a memorable day for
Franks and Danes alike and causing the sun to rise on the
events of the next morning without further ado. The hunt
takes place on an island in the Rhine, to which the company repairs in a pale imitation of the hunting procession
in *Karolus Magnus.* The chief focus of the hunt is on the
extent of the slaughter, and when Prince Lothar is said to
have laid low numerous bears (v. 2391), we are reminded
of Siegfried's supernatural feats in the Black Forest.

The most glaring lapse in poetic tact is the role assigned
to Prince Charles (later Charles the Bald), aged five, in imitation of Ascanius' ornamental role in the Carthaginian
hunt. Whereas Ascanius sheds grace and humor on the
scene, rushing about in high spirits and hoping elatedly
for a boar or a lion, an encounter which luckily does not
come to pass, Ermoldus feels obligated to give Charles a
real part in the hunt. Since he is too young to ride, courtiers are dispatched to capture a fawn for him to strike with
his miniature arms, thus earning a fulsome comparison to
Apollo (vv. 2408–15). We may contrast the crudity of the
passage to Virgil's delicacy in curtailing Ascanius' first experience of war (9. 590–656) and paraphrase Sainte-Beuve's
comment on this latter episode: "Charles est trop jeune
pour la chasse: si jeune, on devient aisément cruel." [10]

The hunting sequence is crowned, as in *Karolus Magnus
et Leo Papa,* by a picnic in a grove, at which Louis and the
youth of the court lounge on seats in the green grass (vv.

[10] *Etude sur Virgile suivie d'une étude sur Quintus de Smyrne,* 3d ed.
(Paris, 1878), p. 178: "Ascagne est trop jeune pour la guerre: si jeune, on
devient aisément cruel."

2422–23, 2428), just as Aeneas and his men are placed on grassy seats in Evander's grove (8. 176); it concludes with a thin echo (v. 2432: *Aufugit acta fames dapibus*) of Virgils' boldly Homeric *Postquam exempta fames et amor compressus edendi* (8. 184).

Ermoldus was the weakest of imitators, and his method consisted chiefly of quarrying the *Aeneid* for narrative situations. Nevertheless, the Virgilian model was so strong that Ermoldus could not altogether escape the old scenic techniques. This is particularly true of the way in which he details a location (Louis' palace or the island in the Rhine) before it comes into play, and the way in which he describes the approaching Danish fleet as it is observed from a distance.

Waltharius

Unlike Ermoldus' feeble effort, the *Waltharius*, a hexameter poem of 1,456 verses, is remarkably independent both in the selection and the treatment of its subject. It is projected against the background of Attila's conquests in central Europe, specifically incursions against Frankland, Burgundy, and Aquitania, which reduce these territories to tributary status. The subjugation is guaranteed by the surrender of hostages to Attila in the persons of the Frankish vassal Hagano (because King Gibicho's son Guntharius is too young), the Burgundian princess Hiltgunt, and the Aquitanian prince Walter. Hagano eventually escapes and returns home, but Walter and Hiltgunt come of age as favored members of the Hunnish retinue. In this shared exile their attachment to one another grows and at length they declare themselves, all the more readily because their parents had intended their union. At the same time, they plan their escape, which is to take place after Walter has organized a splendid banquet and overwhelmed Attila and his court with drink. The plan succeeds, and the couple escape with a considerable treasure.

All goes well until King Guntharius, who has in the meantime succeeded his father Gibicho on the Frankish throne, is made aware of their passage through his realm and determines to seize their gold. He sets out with twelve companions and a reluctant Hagano (who declines to participate in the attack because of his earlier companionship with Walter at Attila's court) and intercepts the fugitives in a narrow defile in the Vosges Mountains. Walter defends the defile against each warrior in succession, killing one after the other until only Guntharius and Hagano remain. At this point Guntharius finally prevails on Hagano to join the fray because he has lost a nephew in one of the preceding encounters. Hagano suggests, however, that they feign withdrawal in order to lure Walter into the open where they can both attack him. Walter suspects as much and cautiously spends the night in his inaccessible lair, but the next morning he ventures forth and is ambushed. The fighting is protracted and ends in a three-cornered draw after Guntharius has lost a leg, Hagano an eye and some teeth, and Walter a hand. The concluding scene finds Walter and Hagano engaging in some incongruous but conciliatory banter about each other's wounds, after which they disperse and, we are told, Walter reigns happily for thirty years wed to Hiltgunt.

The indications within the poem and those available in related texts are not sufficient to tell us what part of this story was in the German model and what part is the poet's elaboration. But what we know of Germanic heroic poetry generally suggests that the model was brief (a couple of hundred alliterative long lines) and chiefly concerned with the direct confrontation between Walter and his attackers.

The Germanic heroic lay normally concludes tragically with the death of one or more of the contestants, but there is no room for such a conclusion in this episode: Hagano and Guntharius must be saved for Kriemhilt's revenge as described in the *Nibelungenlied* or Attila's perfidy as described in the *Edda*. Nor is there any suggestion that Walter succumbed in an earlier version. Perhaps we must assume that the story of Walter was the comedy in the heroic poet's repertory and that it ended on a conciliatory note after the hero's demonstration of prowess.

We can be certain that, whatever the content of the German lay, it paid very little attention to scenery. This is to some extent in the nature of the short form and is also confirmed by the extant remnants of heroic poetry. The lone German fragment from the period, the *Hildebrandslied,* corresponds to the *Waltharius* insofar as it centers on a passage at arms, but the one and only hint of the location is the half line *untar heriun tuem* ("between two armies"). It is therefore particularly instructive to observe how a poet of the Virgilian school elaborates in the area of scenery.

A passage from Walter's days at the Hunnish court as Attila's military commander may serve as a provisory illustration. In these lines Walter leads his troops into battle against an unidentified enemy (vv. 179–206): [11]

> Nec mora, consurgit sequiturque exercitus omnis.
> Ecce locum pugnae conspexerat et numeratam
> Per latos aciem campos digessit et agros.

11 See Hans Wagner, *Ekkehard und Vergil: Eine vergleichende Interpretation der Kampfschilderungen im Waltharius,* Quellen und Studien zur Geschichte und Kultur des Altertums und des Mittelalters, Reihe D: Untersuchungen und Mitteilungen 9 (Heidelberg: Im Selbstverlag von F. Bilabel, 1939), pp. 5–8; Karl Strecker, "Vorbemerkungen zur Ausgabe des Waltharius," *Deutsches Archiv für Geschichte des Mittelalters,* 5 (1941), 43–44 [rpt. in *Waltharius und Walthersage,* pp. 1–32 (see pp. 21–22)]; Wolfram von den Steinen, "Der Waltharius und sein Dichter," *Zeitschrift für deutsches Altertum und deutsche Literatur,* 84 (1952), 28.

Iamque infra iactum teli congressus uterque
Constiterat cuneus: tunc undique clamor ad auras
Tollitur, horrendam confundunt classica vocem,
Continuoque hastae volitant hinc indeque densae.
Fraxinus et cornus ludum miscebat in unum,
Fulminis inque modum cuspis vibrata micabat.
Ac veluti boreae sub tempore nix glomerata
Spargitur, haud aliter saevas iecere sagittas.
Postremum cunctis utroque ex agmine pilis
Absumptis manus ad mucronem vertitur omnis:
Fulmineos promunt enses clipeosque revolvunt,
Concurrunt acies demum pugnamque restaurant.
Pectoribus partim rumpuntur pectora equorum,
Sternitur et quaedam pars duro umbone virorum.
Waltharius tamen in medio furit agmine bello,
Obvia quaeque metens armis ac limite pergens.
Hunc ubi conspiciunt hostes tantas dare strages,
Ac si praesentem metuebant cernere mortem,
Et quemcunque locum, seu dextram sive sinistram,
Waltharius peteret, cuncti mox terga dederunt
Et versis scutis laxisque feruntur habenis.
Tunc imitata ducem gens maxima Pannoniarum
Saevior insurgit caedemque audacior auget,
Deicit obstantes, fugientes proterit usque,
Dum caperet plenum belli sub sorte triumphum.

(Without delay the whole army arises and follows. Now
he perceived the battle site and spread the ordered lines
over the broad plains and fields. And already the two
phalanxes met and stood within a spear's cast of each
other; then a din mounts in the air on all sides, the
trumpets blend their horrid voices, and immediately the
spears fly in a thick pattern hither and thither. There
was an interplay of ash and cornel spears and the whirl-
ing spearheads flashed like lightning. And as the ac-
cumulated snow is scattered by the north wind, just so
did they loose their savage arrows. Then when all the

spears on both sides were exhausted, hands grasped
swords: they unsheathe their flashing brands and draw
in their shields, the battle lines then rush together and
renew the battle. Here the horses collide head on, there
some of the men are overthrown by hard shield-bosses.
But Walter rages in the center of the battle, mowing the
opposition down with his weapons and pursuing his
path. When the enemy saw him making such carnage
and began to fear instant death, at whatever point
Walter sought out, whether to the right or the left, all
turned in flight and were borne away with shields reversed and loosened reins. Then, emulating their leader,
the great people of the Huns surge forward more
fiercely, increase the slaughter more boldly, throw down
the opposing lines, and trample the fugitives until they
have gained a full triumph in war.)

This is a total battle description and it is constructed in
a clearly analytical way. Walter leads out the army, observes the battle terrain, and deploys his forces broadly
across it. Then the opposing lines advance to within a
spear's cast, shouts are raised, trumpets blare, and the
fighting is initiated with a casting of spears and discharge
of arrows. When the missiles are exhausted, the fighting
continues hand to hand with swords and shields. But
Walter rages in the front rank, mowing down the enemy
and cutting a swath, inspiring fear and flight wherever he
appears, and rousing his followers to emulate him until
victory is complete.

The sequence is deliberately structured: observation, deployment, advance, clamor, engagement from a distance,
hand-to-hand fighting, the leader's personal pre-eminence,
and the rout of the enemy. The lines are primarily pat-
terned on *Aeneid* 11. 697–618, but they echo other passages
in the battle books of the *Aeneid* as well. The poet is not
so much dependent on a single model as on Virgil's general

method of visualization, which determines the viewpoint
and outline of the encounter. The overall awareness of
the battle area is akin to that established at the beginning
of *Aeneid* Book 12 (especially vv. 116–33), and the awareness of strategic deployment is akin to the military con-
siderations revealed during Aeneas' landing with his Etruscan allies in 10. 285–309. The clamor and exchange of
missiles echo Tolumnius' initiation of the final full-scale
engagement in 12. 266–69, and the weather simile combines the sense of this passage (12. 284–85) with the word-
ing of 11. 610. Close fighting succeeds the discharge of
missiles as in 12. 287–310. The clash of cavalry reproduces
11. 614–15 and the clash of shields 12. 712. The leader's
pre-eminence is verbally related to Camilla's performance
in 11.762, but may be equated with any aristeia, particularly those of Aeneas and Turnus. The general effect, however, has relatively little to do with specific echoes. It is the
structural instinct that is Virgilian, particularly the setting
of the scene before it is activated, the alternation of mass
movements and individual feats, and the gradual narrowing of the focus. Thus, we are first given a view of the
terrain as Walter sees it, then of the ranks as they confront
one another, then of the narrowing space as they close.
The perspective shrinks when they clash and intermingle
and again when Walter is singled out of the crowd at the
center of the action.

This passage, doubtless included by the poet to give a
preview of Walter's prowess, is a miniature of Virgilian
perspective. It shows how a poet may deal clearly and in
surveyable fashion with a mass scene, an art which, as the
Homeric counterexample demonstrates, was no inevitable
achievement and which Virgil transmitted to his Carolingian successors along with a stock of incident and phrase.

But Walter's early exploit is no more than an episode and serves only to foreshadow the major confrontation with his Frankish assailants in the Vosges Mountains. In this latter scene we may observe more at leisure and in greater detail the effect of the Virgilian guidelines.

Here, too, the poet's first concern is to set the stage, and he does so with a topography which is a curious pastiche of Virgilian echoes (vv. 489–97):

> Interea vir magnanimus de flumine pergens
> Venerat in saltum iam tum Vosagum vocitatum.
> Nam nemus est ingens, spatiosum, lustra ferarum
> Plurima habens, suetum canibus resonare tubisque.
> Sunt in secessu bini montesque propinqui,
> Inter quos licet angustum specus extat amoenum,
> Non tellure cava factum, sed vertice rupum:
> Apta quidem statio latronibus illa cruentis.
> Angulus hic virides ac vescas gesserat herbas.

(In the meantime the valiant man, proceeding from the river, came to a mountainous region called then as now the Vosges. There is a great and ample wood, housing many lairs of beasts and wont to resound with the baying of dogs and the sound of hunting horns. In a secluded spot there are two mountains close to one another, between which there is a narrow and pleasant cave, not hollowed out in the earth but atop the rocks—an excellent hideout for pitiless robbers. This nook was covered with green and delicate grass.)

The lairs of beasts may be a draft on *Georgics* 2. 471 or on *Karolus Magnus et Leo Papa* v. 270, but the habit of mind involved in animating a wilderness with wildlife and the sounds of the hunt is peculiarly Carolingian (for example, *Karolus Magnus* vv. 137–48 and *In Honorem Hludowici*

vv. 232–33, 747, 1242–43, 1839–47, 2368). The rest of the
passage is more specifically Virgilian. The twin mountains
(*bini montes*) are the twin peaks of the landing at Libya
(1. 162–63) moved inland, a landscape to which the pleasant cave (*specus . . . amoenum*) also belongs (1. 166–68).
The robber's den (*apta quidem statio latronibus*) is the
pirates' nest of Tenedos (2. 23: *statio male fida carinis*),
again moved inland.

That one feature of this interior mountain scene is
taken from a coastal landscape and another from an offshore island is a matter of indifference. It is important only
that the scene have specific visual qualities to give the
reader a sense of the stage on which the coming action will
transpire. The poet achieves this purpose with tolerable
success. The landscape is both impressive by virtue of
mountains and cliffs and attractive by virtue of the pleasant
grotto and the green grass—it holds the reader's eye with
a pattern of steep and recessed lines and a combination of
soft and rugged features. Above all, it is not plain or
monotonous. At the same time, it evokes a variety of emotional sensations by offering the prospect of respite and
security while suggesting the potential danger of robbers
and wild animals. The ambiguous mood thus created is
fully exploited when robbers do materialize in the unexpected persons of Guntharius and his retinue.

This approach allows the poet to establish a focus both
to and from Walter's retreat. As he settles down to sleep,
he instructs Hiltgunt to keep watch (vv. 509–10):

> Nam procul hinc acies potis es transmittere puras.
> Instanter cunctam circa explora regionem.

> (From here you can penetrate with your clear eyes far
> into the distance. Search the whole region round about
> attentively.)

In this way we are given a clear view of the position to be guarded and a clear impression of how it dominates the surrounding countryside. There follows a calculated alternation of viewpoint between the advancing assailants and the watchful prey as yet unaware of the contemplated attack. The alternation creates a rudimentary tension, which has its Virgilian counterpart in the alternation between Trojan camp and Aeneas on his mission to Pallanteum in Books 8–10. In the *Aeneid* we are concerned primarily with the plight of the Trojan camp and the uncertainty of relief. In the *Waltharius* we are concerned to know whether Guntharius will discover his quarry and whether, if he does, his victims will perceive the danger and be able to defend themselves.

The discovery comes when Guntharius sees tracks in the dust (vv. 513–14):

> Ast ubi Guntharius vestigia pulvere vidit,
> Cornipedem rapidum saevis calcaribus urget . . .

> (But when Guntharius sees the tracks in the dust, he urges his swift steed with furious spurs . . .)

The chase is on, but before it concludes, the focus reverts to the quarry, and the same dust that betrayed them now signals the danger as it is kicked up by the Frankish riders and becomes visible to Hiltgunt (vv. 532–33; cf. *Aen.* 8. 593, 9. 33–38, 11. 908–9):

> At procul aspiciens Hiltgunt de vertice montis
> Pulvere sublato venientes sensit . . .

> (But looking out into the distance from the peak of the mountain, Hiltgunt perceived the men coming as the dust was raised . . .)

She awakens Walter and while he arms deliberately in preparation for the attack, we observe the gradual approach through Hiltgunt's eyes. First she makes out in the distance the detachment responsible for the dust cloud (v. 536):

> Eminus illa refert quandam volitare phalangem.

> (She reports that some armed troop is rapidly approaching from afar.)

As the detachment draws nearer, she distinguishes the shining lances and expresses her alarm, assuming that they have been overtaken by Hunnish forces sent out to recapture them (vv. 542–43):

> Comminus ecce coruscantes mulier videt hastas
> Ac stupefacta nimis: 'Hunos hic' inquit 'habemus.'

> (Now near at hand the woman sees flashing spears and greatly astounded she said: "Here we have the Huns.")

The next stage is marked by Walter's ability to see that the horsemen are not Huns, but Franks, and to identify Hagano by his helmet (vv. 555–58):

> 'Non assunt Avares hic, sed Franci nebulones,
> Cultores regionis,' et en galeam Haganonis
> Aspicit et noscens iniunxit talia ridens:
> 'Et meus hic socius Hagano collega veternus.'

> ("These are not the Huns, but the Nibelung Franks, the inhabitants of the region." And he sees the helmet of Hagano and, recognizing it, he laughingly spoke as follows: "This is my friend Hagano, my companion of old.")

With visibility clearly established and the gap closing, the focus shifts again and we are invited to look at Walter from Hagano's perspective (vv. 572–73):

> Ast ubi Waltharium tali statione receptum
> Conspexit Hagano . . .

> (But when Hagano saw Walter thus posted . . .)

The distance separating the antagonists is completely obliterated when Guntharius dispatches a spokesman to confront Walter face to face and demand the surrender of the treasure (v. 586):

> Transcurrit spatium campi iuvenique propinquat . . .

> (He traverses the open field and approaches the young man . . .)

Walter naturally refuses, and the assault is imminent. Hagano continues in his fruitless efforts to dissuade Guntharius from the attack and, having failed, he disassociates himself from the enterprise by sitting down on a hill to watch (vv. 638–39):

> Dixerat et collem petiit mox ipse propinquum
> Descendensque ab equo consedit et aspicit illo.

> (Thus he spoke and sought out a nearby hill and, dismounting from his horse, he sat down and observed from it.)

The following sequence of duels gives the illusion of being enacted from the perspective of Hagano sitting at a distance and surveying the scene, or from the perspective of Guntharius as he dispatches one ill-fated retainer after another. This viewpoint is not allowed to slip and is kept before the reader by periodic reminders. Thus Guntharius' view is focused in vv. 720–21 and 754–55:

> Hunc ubi Guntharius conspexit obisse superbus,
> Hortatur socios pugnam renovare furentes.

(When proud Guntharius saw him die, he admonished his furious companions to renew the battle.)

Sed non dementem tria visa cadavera terrent
Guntharium: iubet ad mortem properare vicissim.

(But the view of three corpses does not dismay Guntharius in his madness; he orders his men to hasten to death one after the other.)

The view can be transferred to the Franks as a group (vv. 829–30):

Mirantur Franci, quod non lassesceret heros
Waltharius, cui nulla quies spatiumve dabatur.

(The Franks are amazed that there is no sign of tiring in the champion Walter, to whom no peace or respite was given.)

Or the perspective can be Hagano's, especially when his rash nephew Patavrid is about to charge the indomitable Walter (vv. 847–49):

quem dum procedere vidit,
Vocibus et precibus conatur avunculus inde
Flectere . . .

(When he saw him advance, his uncle tried with words and entreaties to dissuade him . . .)

From the opposite perspective, Walter is aware of this exchange and of Hagano's alarm, despite the intervening distance (vv. 878–79):

Waltharius, licet alonge, socium fore maestum
Attendit, clamorque simul pervenit ad aures.

(Walter, although far off, perceives that his companion
is grieved and the clamor reaches his ears.)

Even Hiltgunt's perspective from behind Walter is maintained in a delicate passage, in which a spear aimed at
Walter overshoots the mark and comes to earth at her feet,
setting her heart aflutter (vv. 891–94):

> In castrum venit atque pedes stetit ante puellae.
> Ipsa metu perculsa sonum prompsit muliebrem.
> At postquam tenuis redit in praecordia sanguis,
> Paulum suspiciens spectat, num viveret heros.

> (It flew into the recess and stuck before the girl's very
> feet. Gripped by fear, she gave a little cry. But after the
> timid blood returns to her heart, she looks up a little to
> see whether the champion still lives.)

Throughout the battle sequence an appreciation of the
distances and perspectives is maintained. All the participants (and nonparticipants) are kept in focus, and some
attention is given not only to their spatial relationships,
but also to their emotional responses: Guntharius' in-
temperance and greed, as well as the weakness reflected by
his dependence on his retainers; Hagano's loyalty and his
futile diplomacy in trying to mediate the confrontation;
Hiltgunt's apprehension for her betrothed; and Walter's
granite spirit tempered by his willingness to make reason-
able concessions in the form of passage money and his
eagerness to avoid the combat with Hagano's nephew
Patavrid, whether out of loyalty to his companion or a
prudent wish not to jeopardize his neutrality or both. The
spatial distribution of Guntharius at a safe distance,
Hagano demonstratively seated apart from the action,
Hiltgunt cowering behind Walter in a recess, and Walter

himself immovable at the center of the scene in what we
must imagine as a narrow defile—all these positions have
psychological as well as scenic functions.

Not only is the personal configuration well focused. The
poet is also at pains to keep the natural setting in view
during the action. The grassy plot behind Walter comes
into view as he drives a captured horse "behind him into
the grass" (v. 780). Some of the surrounding underbrush
appears as an opponent's sword flies out of his hand and
lands in the brambles (v. 836: *procul in dumis resplenduit
ensis*) or when Walter drops his own bloody sword in the
green sedge in order to retrieve his spear (v. 922: *sanguine-
umque ulva viridi dimiserat ensem*). The narrow passage
which Walter defends is variously described as *angusta
callis* (v. 916) and *semita* (v. 957). Finally, the whole
natural scene participates when the mountains are stunned
(v. 823: *stupuit Vosegus haec fulmina et ictus*) or the glen
echoes (v. 996: *saltusque resultat;* cf. *Aen.* 7. 515, 9. 504,
12. 722, 756–57, 928–29).

To sum up, the *Waltharius,* to an even greater extent
than the preceding panegyric poems, has a detailed man-
agement of space and viewpoint. It is not difficult to argue
that this is a Virgilian habit in the case of poets who betray
their indebtedness to Virgil every few lines. But it becomes
more difficult when we abandon the familiar confines of
the Latin tradition to look for traces of Virgilian perspective in the work of a vernacular poet whose acquaintance
with Virgil is disputed. This problem confronts us as we
turn to *Beowulf.*

The Virgilian Heritage
in *Beowulf*

The dating of *Beowulf* is not certain, but scholarly consensus places it in the eighth century. If this dating is correct, *Beowulf* should have been considered before the ninth-century poems surveyed above. I have reversed the probable chronology in order to establish a clear model of Virgilian influence before proceeding to a much less clearcut case. Carolingian epic thus serves as a control in dealing with the possibility of a Virgilian tradition in Anglo-Saxon epic.

Speculation about Virgilian influences in *Beowulf* has been long-standing and inconclusive. There is too much evidence to ignore and too little to decide the case to everyone's satisfaction. Earlier in this century the problem was focused in terms of verbal echoes and narrative analogies, but, although a large number of approximate verbal correspondences can be established, they are only approximate and none is close or extended enough to carry real conviction.[1]

1 See G. Zappert, "Virgil's Fortleben im Mittelalter," *Denkschriften der k. Akademie Wien*, Phil.-hist. Cl., 2 (1851), 17–70; Frederick Klaeber, "Aeneis und Beowulf," *Archiv für das Studium der neueren Sprachen und Literaturen*, 126 (1911), 40–48, 339–59; Rudolf Imelmann, *Forschungen zur altenglischen Poesie* (Berlin: Weidmannsche Buchhandlung, 1920), pp. 65, 247, 249, 263, 374–78, 418–19, 466–68; Alois Brandl, "Hercules und Beo-

A more promising comparison was proposed a few years ago by Alistair Campbell.[2] Campbell argued that Beowulf's recapitulation of the swimming contest with Breca is, in narrative terms, analogous to Aeneas' apologue and constitutes a specifically Virgilian transmission; the device could not have been learned from any epic other than the *Aeneid*. I find this line of argument persuasive and propose to deal with the problem from a similar angle. I shall also attempt to isolate Virgilian influence on the basis of affinities in narrative technique and to ascertain whether Virgil's unique sense of scenic design left the same trace in *Beowulf* that it clearly left in Carolingian epic. The question may be tested against two passages which have figured prominently in the Virgilian debate, Beowulf's voyage to Denmark and his adventure in Grendel's mere. The first of these passages has impressed critics as being particularly rich in Aenean echoes (vv. 210–33):

---

wulf," *Sitzungsberichte der Preussischen Akademie der Wissenschaften,* Phil.-hist. Kl. (1928), 161–67 (rpt. in *Forschungen und Charakteristiken* [Berlin and Leipzig: Walter de Gruyter, 1936], pp. 74–81), and "Beowulf-Epos und Aeneis in systematischer Vergleichung," *Archiv für das Studium der neueren Sprachen und Literaturen,* 171 (1937), 161–73; Tom Burns Haber, *A Comparative Study of the* Beowulf *and the* Aeneid (Princeton: Princeton University Press, 1931). The Homeric parallels in *Beowulf* are well summarized by Ingeborg Schröbler, "Beowulf und Homer," *Beiträge zur Geschichte der deutschen Sprache und Literatur,* 63 (1939), 305–46. Differences between Virgilian and Beowulfian scenery are emphasized by Alain Renoir, "The Terror of the Dark Waters: A Note on Virgilian and Beowulfian Techniques," in *The Learned and the Lewed: Studies in Chaucer and Medieval Literature,* Harvard English Studies 5, ed. Larry D. Benson (Cambridge, Mass.: Harvard University Press, 1974), pp. 147–60.

2 Alistair Campbell, "The Use in Beowulf of Earlier Heroic Verse," in *England before the Conquest: Studies in Primary Sources Presented to Dorothy Whitelock,* eds. Peter Clemoes and Kathleen Hughes (Cambridge: Cambridge University Press, 1971), pp. 283–92. See also Campbell's earlier article, "The Old English Epic Style," in *English and Medieval Studies Presented to J. R. R. Tolkien on the Occasion of His Seventieth Birthday,* eds. Norman Davis and C. L. Wrenn (London: George Allen & Unwin, 1962), pp. 13–26.

210 Fyrst forð gewat;   flota wæs on yðum,
bat under beorge.   Beornas gearwe
on stefn stigon,—   streamas wundon,
sund wið sande;   secgas bæron
on bearm nacan   beorhte frætwe,
215 guðsearo geatolic;   guman ut scufon,
weras on wilsið   wudu bundenne.
Gewat þa ofer wægholm   winde gefysed
flota famiheals   fugle gelicost,
oð þæt ymb antid   oþres dogores
220 wundenstefna   gewaden hæfde,
þæt ða liðende   land gesawon,
brimclifu blican,   beorgas steape,
side sænæssas;   þa wæs sund liden,
eoletes æt ende.   Þanon up hraðe
225 Wedera leode   on wang stigon,
sæwudu sældon,—   syrcan hrysedon,
guðgewædo;   Gode þancedon
þæs þe him yþlade   eaðe wurdon.
Þa of wealle geseah   weard Scildinga,
230 se þe holmclifu   healdan scolde,
beran ofer bolcan   beorhte randas,
fyrdsearu fuslicu;   hine fyrwyt bræc
modgehygdum,   hwæt þa men wæron.

210 The time was at hand;   the craft was afloat,
the ship under the cliff.   The readied warriors
went on board—   the currents eddied,
the sea washed the sand;   the men bore
to the boat's hold   bright weapons,
215 magnificent armor;   the men launched it
on its willing way,   the braced wood hull.
It went over the waves   urged on by the wind,
the foamy-prowed vessel,   most like a bird,
until, at the fixed time   of the following day,
220 the curved prow   had covered the distance
and the sailors   saw land,

the shining sea cliffs,   the steep shore line,
the wide promontories;   then the water was traversed,
the sea at an end.   Thence swiftly
225 the men of the Weder-Geats   made their way to land,
moored the ship,   made ready their armor,
their battle dress;   they thanked God
that their sea voyage   had been an easy passage.
They were seen from the wall   by the Scyldings' sentry,
230 appointed to watch   the sea cliffs,
as they bore down the gangway   their bright shields,
their ready battle byrnies;   he was fain to know,
his mind was vigilant,   what men they were.)

The Virgilian material in this passage is uncertain, but the
parallels are not altogether easy to dismiss out of hand.

The location of Beowulf's ship "under the cliff" (v. 211)
recalls the construction of the Trojan fleet *sub ipsa An-
tandro et Phrygiae . . . montibus Idae* (3. 5–6), and the
loading of armor (vv. 213–15) recalls Helenus' parting gifts
to Aeneas (3. 465–69, cf. *Beowulf* vv. 1896–99):

> . . . stipatque carinis
> ingens argentum Dodonaeosque lebetas,
> loricam consertam hamis auroque trilicem,
> et conum insignis galeae cristasque comantis,
> arma Neoptolemi.

> (. . . and he loads onto the ships a great quantity of
> silver and Dodonaean cauldrons, a battle dress joined
> with hooks and wrought of three-layered gold, and the
> cone of a magnificent helmet and waving plumes, the
> arms of Neoptolemus.)

The wind-impelled, foamy-prowed progress over the water
is the most tempting reminiscence of all. Indeed, the combination of favorable wind and foamy prow as the primary
characteristics of a sea voyage goes back to the *Iliad*
1. 480–82:

They stepped the mast and spread the white sails,
And the wind blew in the center of the sail, and around
The prow of the even vessel the dark swell sounded
   loudly.

Virgil most nearly reproduces the combination in 3. 268–69:

tendunt uela Noti: fugimus spumantibus undis
qua cursum uentusque gubernatorque uocabat.

(The winds spread the sails; we skimmed through foam-
ing waves where the wind and the helmsman guided the
course.)

But the impelling wind may be found also in 1. 524 or
3. 356–57 (whence borrowed by Ermoldus in v. 2506) and
the foam in 1. 35, 9. 103, or 10. 212. The bird simile (v.
218: *fugle gelicost*) echoes Virgil's *aui similis* (4. 254 = *Od*.
5. 51) or, with the superlative, the curious apparition of
Creusa in 2. 794 (*uolucrique simillima somno;* applied to
Anchises' ghost in 6. 702).

The arrival in Denmark (vv. 221–28) suggests a blending
of *Aeneid* 1. 162–73 and 3. 271–77. The steep cliffs (*beorgas
steape*) recall the double cliffs in the Libyan harbor (1.
162–63), which also caught the imagination of the *Waltharius* poet (v. 493), but the sighting of them from open
water is more akin to 3. 270–75:

iam medio apparet fluctu nemorosa Zacynthos
Dulichiumque Sameque et Neritos ardua saxis.
effugimus scopulos Ithacae, Laertia regna,
et terram altricem saeui exsecramur Vlixi.
mox et Leucatae nimbosa cacumina montis
et formidatus nautis aperitur Apollo.

(Then there appears in the midst of the waves woody
Zacynthos and Dulichium and Same and Neritos steep

with rocks. We flee the cliffs of Ithaca, the Laertian realm, and curse the soaring land of savage Ulysses. Then the cloudy mountaintops of Leucates appear and the awesome temple of Apollo is revealed to the sailors.)

The landing and mooring of Beowulf's ship (vv. 225–26) recall the arrival at Actium in the same passage (3. 277):

ancora de prora iacitur, stant litore puppes.

(The anchors are cast from the prows and the hulls rest on the shore.)

On the other hand, the thanksgiving in *Beowulf* (vv. 227–28), which scarcely seems called for after the smooth passage across the Øresund, may have been inspired by the very real sense of relief and escape experienced by the Trojans when they land in Libya (1. 171–73). Finally, the observation of the Geats by a lookout posted on some sort of bluff is reminiscent of Acestes' view of Aeneas and his companions when they return to Drepanum (5. 35–36):

At procul ex celso miratus uertice montis
aduentum sociasque rates occurrit Acestes.

(And from afar atop the high ridge of a mountain, Acestes, marveling at the arrival and the formation of ships, runs toward them.)

In this way we may claim no fewer than nine Virgilian echoes in a passage of twenty-four lines in *Beowulf*. But neither singly nor in combination are these echoes more than a hint; they do not persuade me entirely, nor are they likely to persuade the reader. There is nothing in them that cannot be explained by the commonplaces of sea voyages and landings. Even in the case of the closest analogy, some combination of wind and foam might be expected to occur in any description of the sea.

A large part of the difficulty is linguistic. If the *Waltharius* poet had written in German and borrowed Virgil's Libyan cliffs, they would not have been recognizable. The loan can be detected only because the Latin phrasing gives it away, even though the mountains have been transplanted and are no longer part of a coastal scene. If the *Beowulf* poet had written in Latin, perhaps his phrasing would have betrayed the same loan. We cannot be certain. Broader tests, such as a general comparison of scenic devices, may prove useful in deciding the issue.

We should observe first that the scene of Beowulf's crossing to Denmark is accidented in the Virgilian manner. The departing ship is located beneath an overhanging cliff, and it approaches a terrain characterized by steep cliffs and broad promontories. This view recreates in a rudimentary way the interplay of landscape lines cultivated by Virgil; it is the same sort of articulation we found in the hunting scenery of *Karolus Magnus et Leo Papa* or the secluded defile in the *Waltharius,* landscapes clearly dependent on the Virgilian model. We may also note that the rising cliff landscape is used to provide a broad outlook over the scene. Just as Aeneas climbs a cliff to gain a wider view of the sea off Libya (1. 180), or Misenus is posted on the heights to give warning of the Harpies' swoop (3. 239), or Pallas observes Aeneas' approach up the Tiber from a rise (8. 112), or Charlemagne surveys the construction of Aachen from a citadel (*Karolus Magnus* v. 97), or Louis the Pious observes King Harald's progress up the Rhine *ab excelsa arce* (*In Honorem Hludowici* v. 2175), or Hagano retires to witness the battle from a hill (*Waltharius* v. 638), so the Danish sentry espies Beowulf's arrival from his vantage point *of wealle.*

Beyond the actual deployment of an accidented topography, we have learned to associate the exploitation of varied levels and alternation of focus between those approaching and those observing with Virgilian practice. This alternation obtains when Aeneas catches sight of the walls of Pallanteum and is then observed by Pallas, or when Walter watches the approach of the Franks and is in turn observed by Hagano. In the present instance, Beowulf first sees the shape of the Danish coastline and then becomes visible himself to the coast guard. True to Virgilian precedent, the sightings are registered as full impressions in the eyes of the viewers. The coastal view opens before the ship's crew as a shimmering of cliffs (*land gesawon* / *brimclifu blican*) as the mouth of the Tiber opens up before Aeneas and his men (7. 29–30). From the opposite perspective, the unloading of the ship is visualized through the eyes of the sentry, as the refitting of Aeneas' fleet on the Carthaginian shore is viewed from afar by Dido (4. 408–11). These are some of the scenic techniques I have tried to isolate as specifically Virgilian and not as the property of epic in general.

The whole concept of an articulated sea voyage, in which departure, passage, and arrival are described with some deliberateness, is Virgilian. Homeric displacements are schematic, noting only the points of departure and arrival and making no attempt to develop the intervening distance. Only in the *Aeneid* does travel become palpable in terms of time marked by scenic and emotional factors. There is something fleeting and unreal about the legs of Odysseus' voyage—the intensity of his experience is reserved for dry land. Thus the exhaustion and privation of his eighteen days at sea are brought home to us only at the moment of his collapse on the beach of Scheria. Virgil provides a fuller sea sense, especially in Book 3, where details of departures, arrivals, and sightings while at sea give

an impression of distance and variety wanting in the
Homeric model. This fuller Virgilian experience of the
seascape, on a reduced scale, characterizes Beowulf's crossing to Denmark.

The second passage of particular interest is the march
to Grendel's mere and Beowulf's encounter with Grendel's
mother in her submarine hall (vv. 1399–1650). The landscape through which the Geats approach the mere is
described as follows (vv. 1408–17):

	Ofereode þa	æþelinga bearn
	steap stanhliðo,	stige nearwe,
1410	enge anpaðas,	uncuð gelad,
	neowle næssas,	nicorhusa fela;
	he feara sum	beforan gengde
	wisra monna	wong sceawian,
	oþ þæt he færinga	fyrgenbeamas
1415	ofer harne stan	hleonian funde,
	wynleasne wudu;	wæter under stod
	dreorig ond gedrefed.	

	(The noble youths	made their way across
	steep rocky heights,	narrow paths,
1410	tight defiles,	strange terrain,
	precipitous bluffs,	many dens of monsters;
	one of their number,	of the vigilant men,
	went in advance	to survey the country
	and suddenly found	mountain trees
1415	hanging over	a gray rock,
	a cheerless wood;	water lay below
	bloody and turbid.)	

It has been pointed out that the opening lines bear a resemblance to Virgil's ambush landscape in 11. 524–27: [3]

> . . . tenuis quo semita ducit
> angustaeque ferunt fauces aditusque maligni.

[3] Imelmann, *Forschungen*, pp. 418–19.

> hanc super in speculis summoque in uertice montis
> planities ignota iacet tutique receptus . . .

> (. . . into which leads a narrow path and tight walls
> and a menacing access. Above it on the heights and the
> very summit of the rise there lies an invisible plateau
> and a safe gathering place . . .)

The *stige nearwe* and *enge anpaðas* correspond to Virgil's
semita tenuis and *angustae fauces,* the *uncuð gelad* is the
planities ignota, and the *neowle næssas* are the *speculae.*
On the other hand, Beowulf's tracking of Grendel and his
dam through a wild mountainous region is also reminiscent
of Hercules' tracking of the monster Cacus to his den in
8. 221 (cf. 11. 513–14):

> . . . et aërii cursu petit ardua montis.

> (. . . and he climbs the steep slopes of the soaring moun-
> tain.)

This parallel is attractive because it is supported by the
track which Cacus' stolen cattle leave behind and which
leads to his refuge (8. 209–11). In *Beowulf* the visible
tracks left by Grendel's dam lead to the mere (vv. 1402–4):

> Lastas wæron
> æfter waldswaþum   wide gesyne,
> gang ofer grundas,   . . .

> (Her footprints were
> on the forest track   clear to see,
> her path over the ground,   . . .)

The features of the mere itself have been compared with
certain details of Virgil's underworld landscape in Book

6.[4] The cheerless wood and turbid water are reminiscent of the *tenebrae nemorum* and *niger lacus* (6. 238) which guard the Sybil's cave, and the turbid water has its exact counterpart in the *turbidus gurges* of Acheron (6. 296).

As they continue their march, the Danes pass the head of their companion Æschere abandoned by Grendel's mother and come to a halt by the mere, in which they see and shoot at an assortment of monsters. Beowulf then makes ready for the contest, dives below the surface, and comes to grips with the troll-wife in her hall, a sequence which has its analogy not only in the well-known folktale, but in general terms also in Hercules' penetration of Cacus' subterranean cave. While the prolonged battle is in progress, the Danes and Beowulf's Geat companions sit by the mere and watch the water in anticipation of the hero's reappearance. Eventually the Danes give up hope and return home, but the Geats wait on, sick at heart (vv. 1602–5):

> Gistas setan
> modes seoce   ond on mere staredon;
> wiston ond ne wendon,   þæt hie heora winedrihten
> selfne gesawon.

> (The foreigners sat
> sick at heart   and stared at the mere;
> they wished but weened not   that they would see
> their dear lord again.)

The pathos is reminiscent of two passages in the First *Aeneid* (180–83 and 216–19):

> Aeneas scopulum interea conscendit, et omnem
> prospectum late pelago petit, Anthea si quem

[4] *Beowulf and the Fight at Finnsburg,* ed. Fr. Klaeber, 3d ed. (Boston: D. C. Heath, 1950), p. 183.

iactatum uento uideat Phrygiasque biremis
aut Capyn aut celsis in puppibus arma Caici.

(In the meantime Aeneas climbs the crest and searches
the whole expanse of the sea on the chance that he might
discover Antheas tossed by the wind and the Trojan
ships, or Capyn, or the arms of Caicus in the lofty vessels.)

postquam exempta fames epulis mensaeque remotae,
amissos longo socios sermone requirunt,
spemque metumque inter dubii, seu uiuere credant
siue extrema pati nec iam exaudire uocatos.

(After their hunger was satisfied and the tables removed,
they debate at length the fate of their lost companions,
suspended between hope and fear, not knowing whether
to believe that they are alive or have suffered death and
are beyond recall.)

The scanning of the water and the suspension between hope
and fear suggest an analogy to the attitude of Beowulf's
companions by Grendel's mere.

As in the earlier passage, the specific Virgilian parallels
are tempting if not compelling. But once again the overall
design of the sequence seems difficult to imagine without a
Virgilian background. Nothing in the Germanic material
points to such scenic fullness. Germanic heroic poetry is
free of natural scenery, and even as late as the Icelandic
saga, including the familiar *Beowulf* analogue in *Grettis
saga,* there is no attempt to landscape an encounter in such
detail. The obvious analogy is the *Waltharius,* with its
clear Virgilian etiology and its elaborately developed
setting for a heroic contest.

Like the *Waltharius, Beowulf* dwells at some length on
the journey to the battle site. There is a deliberate account-

ing of the march, a sense of the time consumed, the distance covered, and the countryside traversed. This is the
same sort of perception conveyed by Aeneas' voyages or his
trip up the Tiber to Evander's realm. The surrounding
terrain is characterized chiefly by its steepness, the feature
Virgil uses repeatedly to profile his landscapes, whether in
the departure from Ida, the landward view of mountainous
islands, the arrival in Libya, the survey of Carthage,
Evander's panorama of Rome, or the setting of Turnus'
ambush. This fondness for heights plainly carries over to
the *Waltharius* and may explain the Danish sea cliffs in
Beowulf as well as the steep approach to Grendel's mere.
The immediate verbal echoes in the mere landscape hark
back to Virgil's underworld, and the analogy is reinforced
in more general terms by the obvious attempt to convey a
dismal and chilling atmosphere. The effect is familiar to
the modern reader from *Paradise Lost,* and conscious effort
is required to remember that it is not an inherent part of
epic. Landscape mood was foreign to Homer and is one of
the specifically Virgilian additions to the resources of epic
poetry, not only the eerie Hades of Book 6, but also the
sinister presence of Tenedos, the cataclysm of Troy, the
fearful sight of Etna, the secure refuge in the Libyan harbor, the sense of industry in rising Carthage, the emotional
release of the hunt, or the idyllic vision of Evander's
Arcadia. We have seen how the *Waltharius* poet combined
the threat of Tenedos with the security of the Libyan
harbor to create an ambiguous mood in his epic, and it is
difficult to suppose that the *Beowulf* poet's dreary picture
of Grendel's mere does not owe something to the same
Virgilian tradition of scenic atmosphere.

The final point concerns the use of audience participation. I have indicated what Virgil, unlike Homer, achieves
by visualizing certain scenes through the eyes of an on-

looker or onlookers. The effect can be purely panoramic as
in the audience appreciation of the boat race in Book 5.
But it can also be psychologically complex, as when
Aeneas overlooks Carthage and admits us to the inner experience of what the future may hold for him as well as
the visual experience of what lies before his eyes; or when,
from within his protective cloud, he observes the arrival
of Ilioneus and allows us to appreciate not only the diplomatic exchange between Ilioneus and Dido, but also his
own joy at the unexpected return of his lost companion;
or, again, when Virgil carefully establishes the viewer's
perspective for the culminating duel between Aeneas and
Turnus, a perspective suggesting that Latins and Trojans
alike hang on the outcome because it involves their own
future and the future of Italy as well as the fate of the
participants. The scenic consciousness in this last episode
goes much beyond the relatively isolated duel fought by
Hector and Achilles in the *Iliad*. Virgil has added a new
sense of personal and social anguish, which, one suspects,
also lies behind Hagano's dilemma as he observes the combat between his companion Walter and the retainers of
his liege lord Guntharius, including his own nephew. The
same anguish causes Hiltgunt to tremble for her betrothed, a gesture which owes more to Juturna's grief at
the fate of her brother in the *Aeneid* than to whatever
German lay may have been known to the *Waltharius* poet.
And, finally, the same anguish inspires the forlorn watch
of Beowulf's companions as he struggles with Grendel's
mother at the bottom of the mere.

   Virgilian influence on *Beowulf* is not proved from phrasing alone, but the factors of scenic visualization, deliberate
plotting of space and terrain, the creation of mood, and
the conveying of sensibility through the use of audience
perspective suggest that the *Beowulf* poet was not less

beholden to the scenic techniques of Virgilian epic than were the Carolingian imitators discussed earlier. We will see that these techniques did not necessarily impose themselves when we observe in the next chapter that Virgil's scenic sense, for whatever reason, died in the twelfth century even though the *Aeneid* was taken over directly into vernacular literature and served to some extent as a point of departure for medieval romance.

Vanishing Perspectives
in Medieval Romance

To say that medieval romances have few great scenes is not to diminish them. Indeed, part of their charm is that they flow evenly and nowhere rise in emotional crests. They temper anguished moments by maintaining a deceptive equanimity and declining to reach into the experience. The lovesickness of Lavinie in the *Roman d'Eneas* is superficial and subject to remedy; it is not the fathomless sickness of Virgil's Dido or Tennyson's Elaine. The madness of Chrétien's Yvain or Hartmann's Iwein is largely mimicry, and only Tennyson's Lancelot becomes truly problematical, with a countenance marked to show it.

Impassivity is by no means inherent in medieval style. Where native heroic traditions persist, medieval epic contains memorable scenes with a strong emotional impact, as in the *Chanson de Roland,* the heroic poetry and sagas of Scandinavia, and even the hybrid *Nibelungenlied.* Smooth surface and scenic forbearance are therefore specifically characteristic of the romance, despite the fact that this form begins with and to some extent grows out of an adaptation of the scenically rich and dramatic *Aeneid*— the *Roman d'Eneas,* in which French romance is rooted, and Heinrich von Veldeke's *Eneide,* which exercised a similarly formative influence on the development of German romance. These poems provide a direct link between classical epic and medieval romance and allow us to study by immediate comparison what happens to the scenic tradition as it passes into the vernacular narrative of the High Middle Ages.

The author of the *Roman d'Eneas* avoids Virgil's plunge *in medias res* and begins at the beginning with the sack of Troy and the Trojan departure from Asia Minor. What becomes of the macabre scenery in which Virgil cloaks these events, the silent moonlit infiltration of the Greeks, the first ominous murmurings of armed encounter, the night made lurid by flames, the desolate view of the crumbling city from Anchises' roof, the confused mêlée in the shadowy streets, and the eerie withdrawal in the darkness? It is all lost. Eneas' experience of the attack is limited to four verses (28–31):

> Quant il a cele noise oïe,
> si regarda vers lo donjon
> et vit la grant destrucion;
> n'est mervoille s'il ot peor.

> (When he heard this uproar, he looked toward the citadel and saw the great destruction; small wonder that he was afraid.)

The reader may suppose that the details are being reserved for Eneas' recital when he arrives in Carthage, but such is not the case. He reports to Dido only that the slaughter was indescribable and that he could not relate a tenth of it (vv. 1170–72). As for his own role (1177–79): "I saw the great destruction and assembled many of my people; with great difficulty I departed." How amenable are the terrors of romance!

Hardly less depleted is the great storm of the First *Aeneid* (*Eneas*, vv. 188–209):

One day a great tempest assailed him, for the sea was greatly stirred up; the ships begin to toss, there is thunder and rain, wind and lightning, the weather turned very bad; thunderbolts fall thick and fast, the sea is greatly troubled. Darkness falls and they see nothing; they do not know how to hold their course and they see neither clearing nor sun. They are at a loss: they see no port in any direction and sky and sea threaten death. They see neither moon nor stars; the ropes snap, the sails collapse, mast and rudder split. They suffer much damage and travail. Neither seaman nor helmsman is certain of the right course; they do not know in what direction they are headed, whether they are sailing forward or backward. They have put their lives in peril.

There is something about this description that makes the peril unimpressive, and it is not only the unaspiring diction. The dilution of the model lies partly in the elimination of the Virgilian contrast between an untroubled sea at one moment and an unrestrained tumult at the next. Drama is lacking in the French poet's statement that one day a storm was stirred up. Another difference is the absence of a pre-established natural setting. Virgil is able to suggest the vastness of sea and sky in such a way as to reduce the ships and their crews to insignificance and helplessness before the onslaught of the storm. The French poet focuses immediately on Eneas and thereby allows for some illusion of personal control; Eneas is attacked, he is not simply lost in the midst of a natural cataclysm. Only in the medieval version can there be some thought of countermeasures. Virgil's storm-tossed crews are hardly in a position to look for a port or to consider the possibility of holding their course. Finally, the details in the French adaptation are less drastic. There is little trace of the glowering darkness made incandescent by lightning and split by thunderclaps and no trace of the vast surface of rolling waves or the grotesque dislocation of the seas, which are both mountainous and bottomless. Virgil's special scenic effects are sacrificed, and with them go the menacing quality of the experience and the drain on the hero's emotions.

The leveling down of the storm experience reduces the impact of the arrival in Libya from the very outset. The Libyan shore of the French version is not the *optata harena* onto which Virgil's Aeneas struggled *magno amore telluris* with his companions. Nor is it described beforehand with the complex web of details harking back on the one hand to Odysseus' initial fear at the unfamiliar sight of Scheria and suggesting on the other hand the overpowering sense of relief as well as the pleasures and dangers of the amorous idyll with Dido. For this intricate code the medieval poet substitutes a laconic sighting (vv. 270–72): 'Eneas looked up and looked ahead and saw the land of Libya." The description of what he sees is similarly toneless (vv. 280–84): "They find the country very wild. They see no hut or house, no town or city, only woods. But nonetheless, it pleases them greatly. Eneas goes into the forest." As in the storm scene, the only perspective is that of the observers. We see nothing of the scenery until it is seen by the Trojans, and we therefore have no sense of their immersion in a scene with emotional and symbolic values of its own. The only impression registered in the passage is a kind of picturesque wildness, which is reinforced when Eneas tells his comrades (vv. 346–49): "Here is a very strange country. I don't know whether it was ever cultivated or inhabited; I have never seen a wilder one." These words are a generalized reaction to strange surroundings with no relevance to the particular narrative situation.

The poet's failure to articulate Eneas' response to the

Libyan scene persists as he transfers the inland exploration from the hero to ten messengers acting for him. To these men the countryside is strange merely for the sake of strangeness, and the discovery of Carthage has no personal significance (vv. 365–76):

> They roam through valleys and mountains, through woods and fields; as far as they roamed, they saw no one who could tell them anything, nothing that lived nor any beast. They wandered in the forest until they entered a path; from this there led a broad road. The messengers followed the large road, which was wide, until they saw the city of Carthage, where Dido ruled the fortress.

The travelers experience no hilltop revelation and no expression of longing at the sight of rising walls. Indeed, the city appears to be largely completed (despite the mention of construction work in vv. 545–48), so that there can be no view of industrious humanity repairing its past and building its future. The key word is "fortress," and when the poet describes Carthage, his eye lights first on the natural and man-made fortifications (vv. 409–16). The further description (vv. 419–548) is magnificent and fantastical to a degree calculated to inspire wonder, though the messengers betray none as they proceed to their inquiries in a neutral tone (vv. 551–59):

> They inquired and asked who ruled the city. They were told that a lady was mistress of all the realm. They inquired where she was and followed the directions. At the castle under the tower they found the queen in the hall amidst her great retinue.

After a gracious reception, the messengers return to Eneas and report in a curious passage reminiscent of the

stock comedy scene in which a master must extract information bit by bit from a servant who has suddenly lost
his tongue (vv. 645–52):

> Qu'avez trové?—Nos bien.—Et coi?
> —Cartage.—Parlastes al roi?
> —Nenil.—Por coi?—N'i a seignor.
> —Coi donc?—Dido maintient l'enor.
> —Parlastes vos o li?—Oïl.
> —Menace nos?—Par foi, nenil.
> —Et que dist donc?—Promet nos bien,
> soiez segurs, mar crembroiz rien.

> (What have you found?—Something good.—What is
> that?—Carthage.—Did you speak to the king?—Not at
> all.—Why?—There is no king.—What then?—Dido is
> the ruler.—Did you speak to her?—Yes.—Does she
> threaten us?—Heavens no.—Then what does she say?—
> She promises us aid, feel perfectly safe and fear nothing.)

If the Virgilian drama has not been shattered already, it
certainly disintegrates here. Gone is not only the significance of Carthage as it is first revealed to Aeneas' eyes, but
also the first breathtaking revelation of Dido and Aeneas
to each other. Their meeting takes place under the most
barren and trivial circumstances of court ceremonial.
Eneas rides into town in a procession, which substitutes
ostentation and gawking admiration for his unheralded
appearance in Virgil's poem (vv. 707–19):

> Men go before him and ride two by two; townsfolk,
> ladies, and knights, both in the streets and in the houses,
> go to marvel at them. It was not necessary to ask who
> was lord of the company: though none of them had been
> told, they all knew the king. Each points him out to the
> next with his finger. He was very handsome and agree-

able to look at, a knight large and strapping. To everyone he seemed the handsomest.

Only Dido's first impression, so central in the *Aeneid,* is
not recorded. She simply emerges from her hall, takes him
by the hand, and leads him to a window niche apart from
the others, where he gives an account of himself. Ascanius
is then dispatched to bring gifts and receives a contagious
kiss from Venus, which he communicates to Dido and his
father on his return. The effect is instantaneous, and all
the damage is done before the lovers sit down to their evening banquet. The passion is not, as in the *Aeneid,* a
subtle fusion of visual and mental impressions (of which
Virgil's Cupid is merely emblematic) and a drawing together as the couple, already predisposed by what they
have learned of each other, find the bond gradually
strengthened while they look at one another and listen to
one another's words. With the *Roman d'Eneas* we have
crossed into the romance world of Isolde's love potion, in
which emotional processes are inscrutable and not subject
to analysis.

This new situation reduces the force of the banquet,
which is described largely in terms of culinary magnifi-
cence (vv. 828–32). The warm brightness which repels the
night around the lovers in the *Aeneid* and draws us into
a charmed circle also succumbs to flat hyperbole (vv. 836–
38): "The hall was very brightly lit. So many candles
burned that even in daylight there would not have been
greater brightness." The seductive quality of Aeneas' recital is lost through a much abbreviated and enfeebled version of the fall of Troy and the total abandonment of the
voyage in the Third *Aeneid.* The suffering and romance
are drained from the hero, and there is hardly enough left
to raise the question of what Dido sees in him. Whereas

Virgil's Aeneas has the resonance of varied and profound experience, which modulates his tale to captivate Dido, his romance counterpart has no fullness of experience to be summoned up and reanimated before the queen. One man has a history which can be conveyed as a sequence of powerful scenes, the other has only a magical attraction.

The hunt in the *Aeneid,* with its ominous brightness and abandon, suffers a similar reduction. In the Carolingian period it retained a strong hold and lent color to the poetic canvases of Virgil's imitators. In the *Roman d'Eneas* the color fades. Both the contained energy of the departure and the regal splendor of Dido's delayed entrance are dissipated as she issues indifferent orders to her huntsmen (vv. 1457–60) and has her apparel described in tiresome detail (vv. 1466–80). Instead of the counterbalancing simile comparing Aeneas to Apollo, a touch which establishes a reciprocity of impressions between the lovers as they set out, the French poet reverts to an earlier Virgilian simile comparing Dido to Diana (vv. 1485–90):

> When he saw the Tyrian lady, he thought it was Diana. She was a very beautiful huntress and looked altogether like a goddess. When he looked at her, love made him change color.

The romance makes everything explicit, but, for all its directness, it tells us less than the original.

In the central books the most striking loss of scenery occurs in the voyages which preface Books 7 and 8. The magical night trip from Cumae to the Tiber survives as follows (vv. 3023–32):

> il traient sus singles et voilez,
> si laissent corre aus estoilles.
> Et nuit et jor ont tant coru,

en Lombardie son venu:
ce est la terre et le païs
que Jupiter lor ot promis.
El toivre ariverent les nez,
il metent jus singles et tres,
aancré sont, mais ne savoient
encor en quel païs estoient.

(They raise their masts and sails and set their course by
the stars. They sailed by night and day until they came
to Italy; this is the land and the country which Jupiter
promised them. The ships arrived at the Tiber, they
lowered their sails and masts, they anchored, but they
did not know yet in what country they were.)

The mention of stars does service for the whole complex
of nighttime effects conjured up by Virgil, while the eerie
transition into dawn as the ships approach the Tiber de-
faults completely. Like Homer, the French poet visualizes
a sea voyage largely in terms of rigging.

The same scenic divestment is apparent in the rework-
ing of Aeneas' passage up the Tiber to Pallanteum. The
passage is explained not by the river god's miraculous con-
cert, but by military operations which have endangered
the overland route and made the river route safer (vv.
4593–94). Thus divine auspices yield to rational causes.
The description of the voyage itself also shrinks the imaginative dimensions and betrays a curious lack of poetic resources by echoing the previous voyage from Cumae (vv.
4609–17):

Tot en plorant son fil besa,
al Toivre vint, es nes antra,
dous an a fait desaancrer.
Il comança a avesprer;
il a fait traire sus les voilles,

la nuit siglerent as estoilles
et l'endemain tot altresi,
jusqu'al tier jor androit midi.
Idonc vindrent soz Palantee;

(Weeping he kissed his son, came to the Tiber, boarded
his ship, and had two of them weigh anchor. Evening
was beginning to fall; he had the sails raised and they
sailed at night by the stars and so onward the next day
until the third day exactly at noon. Thus they arrived
beneath Pallanteum.)

Anchor, sails, stars, and the journey by night and day are
details familiar from the earlier voyage (vv. 3023–32). The
features which distinguished Virgil's treatment of this river
journey, the nighttime quiet and the enveloping nature
along the banks, are retrieved as an afterthought (vv. 4618–
22):

bois a par tote la contree
sor lo Toivre par lo rivage;
il aloient amont a nage,
soz les arbres lo covert tindrent,
tant que desoz la cité vindrent.

(The whole country is wooded along the banks of the
Tiber; they sailed upstream under the cover of the trees
until they arrived beneath the city.)

Here we can look over the shoulder of the French adapter
at work. He recounts the voyage by relying, in formulaic
fashion, on the phrasing evolved in an earlier description
and concludes the passage with the arrival at Pallanteum
(v. 4617). Then he looks back at Virgil and realizes that he
has said nothing about the natural scenery which looms
so large in his model. He therefore retraces his steps and
fills in the wooded banks, ending with a second arrival at

Pallanteum (v. 4622), which simply echoes the previous arrival (v. 4617). Events and surroundings have been allowed to separate, and it seems clear that the imitator has lost all sense of the integration of scene and experience which is a hallmark of Virgil's narrative technique.

In the battle books the changes are analogous. The visual effects in Books 10 and 11 are systematically reduced, and nothing is left of the dramatic concentration and the calculated stripping away of Turnus' surroundings in Book 12. For the sake of a single example from among the battle sequences, we may take the scene of Aeneas' return to his camp in Book 10. Instead of the imposing sight of Aeneas on the stern of his approaching vessel, holding high the flashing shield of Vulcan, we are offered yet another view of rigging (vv. 5602–4):

> Il ont gardé aval al port
> et voient ariver les nes
> et metre jus sigles et tres;

> (They [the defenders of the camp] looked down to the harbor and see the ships arriving and lowering sails and masts.)

The besieged men are overjoyed and shout their approval, providing the adapter with the material for another rational digression. He argues (vv. 5608–18) that they shouted prematurely, thereby forewarning the besieging forces, which otherwise would have been encircled by Eneas' unperceived advance from the rear. This remark deserves a place in the Virgilian commentaries as an unwitting illustration of Virgil's preoccupation with emotional portrayal; according to his interpretation the tension in the camp is so great and Aeneas' appearance such a signal deliverance that the defenders cannot contain their joy. Virgil contrived a picture of desperate men suddenly and miraculously released, not a bungled military maneuver.

One mention of a tactical error does not mean that a sense of military strategy is maintained consistently in the *Roman d'Eneas*. In Virgil's account Turnus carefully divided his forces so as to confront the new danger while maintaining the investment of the camp. In the French version he abandons the siege entirely and rushes down to the ships to join battle with the newcomers. All the details of the landing are dropped, and the fine symbolism of the stubborn battle for the beachhead *in ipso limine Hesperiae* yields to the lines (vv. 5637–40): "All those of the army arrived there and the others emerged from the ships and they began to joust next to the sea on the sand." Faced with the task of describing the general engagement, the adapter subsides into Homeric disconsolateness (vv. 5641–44): "It would be hard to tell everything and account for the jousts, the feats of prowess which each accomplished, who was killed and who killed him." The only escape from the difficulties is into numbers and hyperbole (vv. 5645–46): "But a wondrous number died and the sea is all red from it."

The absence of scenic visualization in the *Roman d'Eneas* is equally characteristic of later romance. But, although the cultivation of scenic and spatial factors is so conspicuously wanting, a good deal of critical attention has been devoted to this aspect of romance narrative technique, more than to the same factors in the classical epic. The material that has been collected is abundant and helpful, but, with incidental exceptions, the problem has not been viewed against the background of classical and earlier medieval epic.

The use to which landscapes are put by the father of medieval romance, Chrétien de Troyes, is the subject of a

study by Manfred Gsteiger.[1] Gsteiger emphasizes typical
features and singles out for synthetic treatment certain set
situations—"Castles and Towns," "The Forest," "Trees,"
"Gardens, Meadows, and Orchards," "Descriptions of
Springtime," "Plain and Field," "Mountains and Valleys,"
"River Landscapes," "The Sea," and "Journeys and Landscape Surveys." Scenes in each category tend to be pat-
terned in similar ways from one passage to the next and
from one romance to the next. Castles are regularly fair
and strong; if they are placed in a surrounding landscape,
they are described as being by a river, on a hill or cliff, by
the sea, on a heath, or in a valley. Attempts at more pre-
cise description are limited to high walls or towers and
deep moats, or, on occasion, the specification of such additional architectural features as gate, drawbridge, outworks,
portcullis, battlements, and courtyard. Only in a couple of
instances in the *Conte du graal* does Chrétien try to convey a special sense of visibility by causing castle towers to
spring up before the eyes of an approaching traveler.

Forests are characteristically deep, dense, broad, and
dark, and they tend to be mentioned either as knights
enter them or emerge from them. They normally function
as haunts for wild animals, as hunting grounds, or as scenes
of adventure, notably ambushes. Specific tree species or
bushy undergrowth are mentioned occasionally, while individual trees may serve the purpose of scenic marking,
rather like the wild fig tree or the oak tree in Homer's
Iliad.[2] Typically, persons are pictured sitting or standing
under such a tree.

Gardens, meadows, and orchards are connected by

[1] *Die Landschaftsschilderungen in den Romanen Chrestiens de Troyes:
Literarische Tradition und künstlerische Gestaltung* (Bern: Francke, 1958).
[2] Gsteiger (p. 28) quotes Ernst Robert Curtius, "Rhetorische Naturschil-
derung im Mittelalter," *Romanische Forschungen*, 56 (1942), 243: "Wie
schon in der Ilias, dienen auch im Rolandslied Bäume zur epischen

Gsteiger with the *locus amoenus* tradition. Pleasant meadows are characterized by clear springs and shady trees and
are sometimes located in a wild forest landscape. Gardens
and orchards are generally located within castle grounds
and can be combined with trees and springs as well as with
meadows. A subvariety is the magical garden with plants
in perpetual bloom. Such landscapes are most frequently
conceived of as backdrops for love scenes.

Plains and fields normally are seen as large, beautiful,
level, broad, or open, and they typically are employed as
battle sites. This appears also to be the chief function of
mountain and valley landscapes, as well as of river and
ford scenes. Most of these and the preceding landscape features also turn up to characterize the natural scenery along
the routes followed by knights errant.

Gsteiger argues that the use of landscape in Chrétien's
romances (along with the *romans d'antiquité* and the *lais*
of Marie de France) represents some progress beyond the
practice in the *chansons de geste* and that the simple mention of landscape features begins to develop into real description. However, against the larger background of
classical epic, this progress seems trifling. Gsteiger devotes
a short chapter (pp. 83–97) to Chrétien's relationship to
classical models (notably Virgil and Ovid), leaving open
the possibility of some direct influence, but the discussion
suffers from an underestimation of the scenic complexities
in Virgil and a restriction of the comparison to the level
of phrase. Tentative efforts are made to identify a drift toward a symbolic use of landscape to evoke mood, but
again, the findings are meager. Landscape features in
Chrétien, by and large, are formulaic and do not have a

Markierung der Landschaft." See also Curtius' essay, "The Ideal Landscape," in *European Literature and the Latin Middle Ages*, trans. Wil-
lard R. Trask (New York: Harper Torchbooks, 1963), pp. 186 and 201.

clearly designed function in promoting visibility or modifying the reader's understanding of the scenes in which they occur.

In an article abstracted from his 1960 Berlin dissertation, Joachim Schildt tried to outline a general development of landscape in the German romance.[3] He distinguished five increasingly complex types of landscape description, which reveal a gradual growth in sophistication over the period from 1050 to 1270.

Tyae 1 (1050 to 1150) comprises simple designations of a landscape by a single noun, which may or may not be modified by adjectives. The noun may designate a total landscape (sea, field, forest, mountain) or an individual feature (olive tree, linden, log, spring). Type 2 (1150 to 1180–1190) provides detail by using a series of nouns, one designating the general scene and the others filling in particular aspects. Type 3 (1180–1190 to 1230–1240) is more nearly descriptive. A scene is established by plotting one basic landscape feature in relation to others through the use of prepositions, adverbs, and verbs compounded with prepositions. Type 4 (also 1180–1190 to 1230–1240) again is descriptive, but interprets the scene by filtering it through the eyes of an observer or by introducing dynamic elements such as motion. Type 5 (1230–1240 to 1250–1270) elaborates on Type 4 by relating the landscape to the person in it, as in the case of the blood drops on the snow that lead Parzival to reflect on Condwîrâmûrs. Parzival's childhood in the forest also belongs to this type since the scene suggests his innocence of worldly matters.[4]

---

[3] "Zur Gestaltung und Funktion der Landschaft in der deutschen Epik des Mittelalters," *Beiträge zur Geschichte der deutschen Sprache und Literatur* (Halle), 86 (1964), 279–307.

[4] Although Schildt's types cover the whole range of German romance, he takes his examples from Wolfram's *Parzival* for the sake of convenience: Type 1 (105. 27–30), Type 2 (58. 2–8), Type 3 (681. 2–17), Type 4 (180. 21–181. 9 and 508. 1–14), Type 5 (282. 1–283. 15). The blood-drop

In addition to the main function of establishing the scene of an episode, these romance landscapes have certain auxiliary functions. The simple landscape designation (Types 1 and 2) often serves to support comparisons or to emphasize the dimensions or the importance of a scene, but the descriptive landscapes (Types 3 to 5) are more versatile in their application. They may contribute to motivation, for example by detailing the construction of a castle in order to stress its impregnability. They may create mood by evoking the unreal features of a fairy-tale landscape. They may be didactic where geographical information appears to be the object. Or, finally, they may mark a resting point or narrative plateau in the sequence of adventures.

The most elaborate treatment of landscape in romance is Ingrid Hahn's study of Gottfried's *Tristan*.[5] Her terminology corresponds in part to Schildt's, but she emphasizes that most of her categories have only a limited application in *Tristan*, where simple designation is the rule and descriptive passages very rare.[6] She finds a conscious suppression of objective reality in comparison to the works of Hartmann von Aue and Wolfram von Eschenbach, and she interprets this discrepancy in terms of Gottfried's internalization of the action.[7] In addition, she introduces certain new categories into her observations: traversed space, visible space, space perceived through the other senses, grouping, progress toward a determined point, and

---

reverie and forest childhood are also singled out of Chrétien's *Conte du graal* by Gsteiger (pp. 115-16 and 122-23) as examples of symbolic landscapes.

[5] *Raum und Landschaft in Gottfrieds Tristan: Ein Beitrag zur Werkdeutung*, Medium Aevum 3 (Munich: Eidos, 1963).

[6] Ibid., p. 40.

[7] Ibid., p. 37. See also Rainer Gruenter, "Zum Problem der Landschaftsdarstellung im höfischen Versroman," *Euphorion*, 56 (1962), 256-57.

the setting in relief of the hero.[8] These categories, as well
as the ones proposed by Schildt, are only partially represented in *Tristan*. The traversed landscape, for example,
is not developed by Gottfried and even where it occurs in
other romances, it visualizes only a narrow strip adjacent
to the traveler, never a broad panorama. Even the mod-
erately elaborate visualization of a castle, which Gsteiger
found in Chrétien and which may be matched in German
romance, has no counterpart in *Tristan*.[9]

Although Hahn does not specifically compare Gottfried's
spatial techniques with those of Virgil, a number of passages and devices are discussed that suggest analogies (and
contrasts) to the *Aeneid*. Most immediately comparable,
perhaps, is the storm sequence that causes the Norwegian
merchants to set Tristan ashore in Cornwall (vv. 2401–
2533):

> In the meantime the Norwegians carried him off and
> might well have managed to fulfill their wishes and in-
> tentions concerning him. But this was countermanded
> by Him who makes all things straight and, by straight-
> ening, corrects them, Whom winds, sea, and all forces
> serve in fearful submissiveness. As He willed and com-
> manded, such an overwhelming storm arose on the sea
> that they could do nothing for their own protection
> other than to let their ship drift wherever the wild
> winds drove it, while they themselves remained uncer-
> tain of life and limb. They had surrendered themselves
> altogether to the frail support of what is called fortune
> and they left it up to chance whether they survived or
> not. For all they could do was to mount up to the
> heavens on the wild sea and then plunge down again as
> if into the abyss. The maddened waves drove them now

---

[8] Hahn, *Raum und Landschaft*, pp. 45–50, 57–60, 60–63, 67–69, 69–70,
83–85.

[9] Ibid., pp. 40–41, and Gruenter, "Zum Problem," pp. 252–57.

up, now down, now hither, now thither. None of them
could hold his footing for any length of time. This was
their situation for eight days and eight nights and with
that they were almost at the end of their strength and
their wits. Now one of them spoke up: "Gentlemen, I do
believe that our fearful situation is God's command; the
explanation for our hovering on the brink of death in
these maddened waves is clearly that we were sinful and
faithless when we abducted Tristan from his family."
"Yes," they all spoke at once, "you are right and it is
so." Then they took counsel and decided that if they
wanted to quiet wind and waves, they should head for
shore and let him go freely wherever he wished. And as
soon as this was done and they were all agreed on this
course of action, their perilous journey was immediately
relieved; winds and waves began to dissolve and subside,
the sea began to settle, and the sun to shine as brightly
as before. Here they did not delay because during the
eight days the wind had driven them to the land of
Cornwall and they were already so close to the shore
that they could see it and they put to shore immediately.
Then they took Tristan and set him ashore and put
bread and some other of their victuals in his hand.
"Friend," they said, "may God give you good fortune
and make you prosper." With this they all gave him
their blessing and departed again. Now what did Tristan
do, Tristan the exile? Well, he sat there and wept because children know only enough to weep when something happens to them. The desolate exile clasped his
hands and raised them fervently to God: "Alas," he said,
"almighty God, I implore you to show me your mercy
and your goodness since you have determined that I
should thus be led astray, and direct me to where I can
again be among human beings. Now I look all about
and see nothing living around me. I fear this great wilderness; wherever I look, the world is closed, and wherever I turn, I see nothing but barren ground and waste

and wilderness, wild cliffs and the wild sea. This fear
besets me and above all I fear that wolves and beasts
will devour me wherever I go. And now the day is declining toward evening; if I wait any longer before leaving this spot, it would be most unwise. If I do not hasten
away soon, I will spend the night in this forest and there
will be no hope for me. Now I see that around me rise
many high cliffs and mountains; I think I will climb one
of them, if I can, and observe, as long as I have daylight,
whether there is any dwelling here either near or far,
where I might find people with whom I can stay and
survive in whatever way possible." Then he got up and
set out.

Incidental details in the stormscape suggest that either
Gottfried or his model Thomas referred directly to the
Aeneid. The waves mounting to the heavens and plunging
into an abyss (vv. 2426–29) recall Virgil's *fluctusque ad
sidera tollit* (1. 103) and *hi summo in fluctu pendent; his
unda dehiscens terram inter fluctus aperit* (1. 106–7), and
the restoration of stillness and sunlight (vv. 2462–65) recalls Virgil's *tumida aequora placat collectasque fugat
nubes solemque reducit* (1. 142–43).[10] If this is so, Gottfried's consistent departure from Virgil's descriptive con-
cepts is all the more remarkable. He gives no picture of
the massing and descent of the storm. It is simply there
by a motion of the divine will. He does not evoke the appearance of sea and sky or attempt to focus the ship or the
ship's company in a larger context; we are left to visualize
the chaos in our own minds. The only movement is up
and down or this way and that, and the only detail that
signals the plight of those on board is their difficulty in
keeping their feet. But despite eight days of unremittent
buffeting, the tone of the council on board gives no hint
of exhaustion or despair. Nor does the sighting of land

10 Hahn, *Raum und Landschaft,* p. 18.

suggest any corresponding relief. As in the *Roman d'Eneas,* the threat of the storm seems unreal because it is described too incompletely and is insufficiently registered on the emotions of the men who are exposed to it.

The approach toward the Cornish coast also suffers from a want of visible detail. The landscape is not focused beforehand and therefore does not relate directly to Tristan's sensations as he sits on the shore. Only in his supplication to God does it become apparent that he has observed the landscape and experienced fear—the spatial dimension is established in retrospect.[11] Landscape features abound (Tristan mentions barren ground, wilderness, waste, wild cliffs and sea, a forest, and, again, high cliffs and mountains), but they are not interrelated and do not coalesce into a picture. We can only determine that the outlook is wild and frightening.[12]

Gottfried unconsciously retreats behind Virgil's descriptive level to a stage represented by the *Odyssey:* like Odysseus, Tristan takes no cognizance of the coast on which he finds refuge until he has landed, like Odysseus he is preoccupied with the fear of wild beasts, and like Odysseus he gazes landward in search of human habitation, not seaward in order to create the spatial totality we observed in the *Aeneid.*

A second example of undervisualized landscape in *Tristan* is the passage in which Mark's hunter comes upon the Cave of Love by following the tracks of a hart which had eluded him on the preceding day (vv. 17,327–46): [13]

> Early the next morning the hunting master set out before he perceived dawn; he told his followers to wait for day and then ride after him. He leashed a hound that

[11] See also Gruenter, "Zum Problem," pp. 257–58.
[12] Hahn, *Raum und Landschaft,* p. 14.
[13] Ibid., pp. 69–70.

suited him and put him on the right track. He led him
forth over much rough terrain, over mountains and over
rocky ways, over arid ground and over grass, where the
hart had fled and escaped during the night. He followed
the track until the defile was at an end and the sun well
over the horizon. Then he had come to the spring on
Tristan's clearing.

The terrain is not very different from Beowulf's trail to
Grendel's mere (vv. 1408–17); in both passages the traveler
crosses difficult ground, steep, rocky, and narrow, and arrives at a particular point, in one case a pool and in the
other a spring. Only the degree of visibility varies. Gottfried once again accumulates general features in order to
suggest the vague outline of a landscape, but the effect is
disorderly and the assembled features are not integrated
into a picture. The alternation of arid and grassy stretches
does not quite make sense, and the defile mentioned at the
end of the passage has not been worked into the previous
landscape. The spring and the clearing at which the hunter
arrives are not focused with any visible characteristics.

The *Beowulf* poet was more consistent. Mountains,
stony path, and narrow defile are all of a piece. The isolation and remoteness of the scene are made graphic by the
"dens of monsters," however apocryphal these may be, and
the impinging landscape is emphasized by the very lack of
visibility implied in the necessity of dispatching a scout to
survey the country ahead. Finally, the arrival is marked by
the "sudden" discovery of a pool, vividly characterized by
overhanging trees, a gray rock, a cheerless wood, and turbid waters. The application of firm contours, as well as
the effective integration of landscape and mood, makes the
Beowulf passage distinctively Virgilian. The absence of
these qualities in *Tristan* is characteristic of the decline in
landscape perspective peculiar to medieval romance.

CHAPTER 6 ❧

Conclusion

The study of medieval epic in recent decades has tended
to emphasize the persistence of the classical tradition,
partly because of Ernst Robert Curtius' pervasive influence and partly because of the comparatist's inclination to
evaluate similarities first and differences later.[1] I have departed from this emphasis in an effort to focus the dis-
continuities as well as the continuities in the development
of epic scenery from Homer to the medieval romance. The
first sharp break in the tradition is clearly Virgil's far-
reaching elaboration of the Homeric model, his detailed
landscapes, his panoramic perspectives, and his creation of
a new emotional density through the use of scenic mood
and the interaction of men and their surroundings. Virgil's
changes produced radically different scenic perceptions,
and part of my task has been to clarify the mechanics of
the metamorphosis. To this extent the book is about Virgil.

The second part of my task concerns the fate of Virgil's
scenic innovations in the medieval period. Here another
important break occurs. Whereas the epic experiments of
Carolingian Germany and Anglo-Saxon England betray

1 A welcome reversal, with which I should like to associate myself, is
Peter Dronke's *Poetic Individuality in the Middle Ages: New Departures
in Poetry 1000–1150* (Oxford: Clarendon, 1970). See especially his program-
matic first chapter, "Poetic Individuality: Questions" (pp. 1–32).

Virgilian scenic conventions as well as phraseology, vernacular romance beginning in the twelfth century ceases
to participate in the tradition. The explanation is to some
extent linguistic. The Carolingians wrote Latin and, in
their attempts to revive the epic, they wrote specifically in
the Virgilian idiom. Naturally enough, their reliance on
Virgilian phrasing brought with it a reliance on Virgilian
technique. But there were considerable variations, depending on the skill of the individual poet. *Karolus Magnus et
Leo Papa* and the *Waltharius* demonstrate an appreciation
of Virgil's larger rhetorical patterns quite beyond the grasp
of the less gifted Ermoldus. Nor is the Carolingian achievement exhausted by referring simply to Virgilian precedent.
Karolus Magnus intensifies scenic effects beyond any specific model in the *Aeneid,* and the *Waltharius* poet demonstrates a remarkable ability to combine and reinterpret
Virgilian methods.

   Beowulf raises special problems and my arguments to
justify a place in the Virgilian tradition may be no more
compelling than others offered long ago. The language of
epic has changed, and the verbal tests fail. Nonetheless,
I hope that I have made it plausible that the scenic consciousness in *Beowulf* bears more than a chance resemblance to the *Aeneid.* If so, the explanation lies not in the
bonds of the Latin language that confined the Carolingian
writers, but in the literary experience of an Anglo-Saxon
poet so steeped in Virgil's epic practices that the master
was not altogether obscured by his disciple's adoption of a
new tongue and a new system of diction.

   The possibility of a direct relationship between the
Aeneid and *Beowulf* is strengthened by the observation
that scenic design of the Virgilian type is by no means a
ubiquitous or inevitable phenomenon to be found indis-
criminately throughout narrative poetry. Virgilian scenery

disappeared in the later Middle Ages and did not survive even when the *Aeneid* itself was converted into the vernacular during the twelfth century. The analysis of how it disappeared is calculated to underscore, by the use of a counterexample, the real affinities between *Beowulf* and the older Virgilian school. This analysis is necessarily negative, but not all genres can be all things. My last chapter should not be construed as a deprecation of romance, but rather as a further step toward the definition of romance, in this case through the study of scenic reductions.[2] Once more it should be apparent that whatever romance is, it is not epic.

2 I have in mind such approaches as Morton W. Bloomfield's "Episodic Motivation and Marvels in Epic and Romance," *Essays and Explorations: Studies in Ideas, Language, and Literature* (Cambridge, Mass.: Harvard University Press, 1970), pp. 97–128.

Index

EARLY EPIC SCENERY

Designed by R. E. Rosenbaum.
Composed by Vail-Ballou Press, Inc.,
in 11 point linotype Baskerville, 2 points leaded,
with display lines in monotype Baskerville.
Printed letterpress from type by Vail-Ballou Press
on Warren's No. 66 text, 50 pound basis.
Bound by Vail-Ballou Press
in Joanna book cloth
and stamped in All Purpose foil.

Library of Congress Cataloging in Publication Data
(For library cataloging purposes only)

Andersson, Theodore Murdock, 1934-
    Early epic scenery.

    Includes bibliographical references and index.
    1. Nature in literature.   2. Epic poetry, Classical—History and criticism.
3. Beowulf.   I. Title.
PA3015.N3A5   809.1'3   76-12593
ISBN 0-8014-1013-4

Date D